A GUIDE TO FORMATION ADVISING
FOR SEMINARIANS

D1479132

A COMPANION TO
A Guide to Formation Advising for Seminary Faculty
by Deacon Edward J. McCormack

A Guide to Formation Advising for Seminarians

Deacon Edward J. McCormack

FOREWORD BY
RONALD D. WITHERUP, PSS

The Catholic University of America Press
Washington, DC

Library of Congress Cataloging-in-Publication Data

Names: McCormack, Edward J., 1960- author.
Title: A guide to formation advising for seminarians / Deacon Edward J. McCormack; foreword by Ronald D. Witherup, PSS.
Description: Washington, D.C. : The Catholic University of America Press, 2020. | Includes bibliographical references and index. | Summary: "Recent Vatican guidelines for seminary formation call for professional accompaniment of seminarians throughout their formation to become Catholic priests. This book lays out what these seminarians should expect from the entire formation process. Written by a veteran formator at a Roman Catholic seminary, it offers a practical guide to formation advising from the point of view of the men who will experience it. It includes a guide to and an example of the self-evaluation that is part of this process. The book contains an index and an annotated bibliography on the main areas of formation relevant to seminarians"—Provided by publisher.
Identifiers: LCCN 2020026699 (print) | LCCN 2020026700 (ebook) | ISBN 9780813233116 (paperback) | ISBN 9780813233123 (ebook)
Subjects: LCSH: Catholic Church—Clergy--Training of. | Catholic theological seminaries. | Priesthood—Catholic Church. | Pastoral theology—Catholic Church.
Classification: LCC BX903 .M3278 2020 (print) | LCC BX903 (ebook) | DDC 230.07/32—dc23
LC record available at https://lccn.loc.gov/2020026699
LC ebook record available at https://lccn.loc.gov/2020026700

To the present and former faculty and seminarians
of Theological College in Washington, DC.

You give me hope for the future of the Church.

Contents

Acknowledgments

DURING MY TWENTY YEARS as a professor of theology and a formation advisor, so many people have been generous to me and supportive of my work and career. I want to thank Robert Leavitt, PSS, who hired me to be a member of the faculty at St. Mary's Seminary and University while I was still completing my dissertation. It was there that I first learned about formation advising. Phillip J. Brown, PSS, supported this project from its inception. I am grateful to Gerald McBrearity, the Rector of Theological College, who has supported this project from beginning to completion. Gerry, David Thayer, PSS, and Jim Froelich, OFM Cap., all read early drafts of the manuscript and provided critical comments that improved the work immensely. Richard Gula, PSS, read through a draft of the manuscript offering careful and critical comments. I am grateful to the time and care he took in reading the entire draft. I have learned so much about forming men for the priesthood from the faculty at Theological College and the many seminarians I have had the privilege to work with over these many years. They give me hope for the future of the Church. I want to thank John Martino and the Catholic University of America Press for their support and guidance throughout this project. Finally, I want to thank my wife and two girls for their presence, support, and love. They make all the work worthwhile.

Foreword

SINCE THE BEGINNING OF his pontifical ministry in March 2013, Pope Francis has made a point of placing priestly formation and priestly ministry and life at the forefront of many of his allocutions. He has warned against the dangers of clericalism and careerism, and he has called attention to formation as a lifelong endeavor. In the first months of his pontificate, while addressing a large group of seminarians, novices, and young people discerning their vocations, the Holy Father reminded them of the importance of "good, balanced formation that unites all the dimensions of life, the human, the spiritual, the intellectual dimension with the pastoral" (July 7, 2013). He encouraged them to embrace their years of formation as "a season of discovery."

For seminarians, however, the world of priestly formation can sometimes be bewildering and uncomfortable. It has its own jargon and methods, and some aspects of formation may strike the newcomer as unnecessarily complicated. It also involves "accompaniment" by experienced formators whose primary task is to ensure that proper vocational discernment happens as one prepares to be ordained. This process, called "advising," entails evaluations at every stage. No one likes to be evaluated. Evaluations can make most of us unsure of ourselves. Yet every seminary formation program is built on the premise of growth and discernment, which can only happen when seminarians honestly embrace the formation process as a grace-filled means of configuring themselves more and more to Jesus Christ, the Good Shepherd. While good self-evaluation is necessary in this process, external objective evaluation is also essential.

This book, written by Deacon Edward McCormack of Theological College of The Catholic University of America in Washington, DC, serves the purpose of priestly formation very well. It provides an essential handbook on accompaniment and formation advising. It is designed to set seminarians at ease as they work their way through multiple obligations during their years of formation. It lays out the step-by-step expectations of priestly formation as enunciated in the most recent document on universal norms for priestly formation, the *Ratio Fundamentalis Formationis Sacerdotalis* (2017) issued by the Congregation for Clergy. The present book takes the principles explained in the *Ratio* and applies them to seminary formation so they can be a valuable resource for every person in seminary formation.

The first part of this handbook clearly enunciates the theoretical foundations of priestly formation, especially in its four dimensions—human, spiritual, intellectual, and pastoral. Succeeding chapters expand the formation process in all its complexity to expose the method and content of each stage of priestly formation as one progresses to the final goal of ordination. At the heart of this approach is the attempt to forge an integrated view of formation that does not compartmentalize each distinctive element. Formation advising has human, spiritual, and intellectual dimensions to it that feed into one's pastoral formation, which is where true integration of all priestly formation should be readily evident ("vocational synthesis" expressed in *Ratio* §74). Ideally, seminarians will foster each aspect of their lives with openness and humility, and they will accept more and more responsibility for their formation as they grow into the "missionary disciples" called for by recent Church teaching. Along the way, this handbook provides concrete guidance about a multitude of pertinent subjects, especially the importance of goal-setting, pastoral reflection, growth in celibate chastity, making the most of self-evaluations, and developing a more self-reflective lifestyle that will lead to the recognition of formation as a lifelong process (*Ratio* §80).

In the name of the Sulpician General Council, I express sincere gratitude to Deacon Edward McCormack for writing this handbook for seminarians in accordance with the Church's most recent teaching on priestly formation. Seminarians who take full advantage of this practical resource should be grateful that they are beneficiaries of a generous, devoted, and talented formation team whose true desire is to see them become the best priests they can possibly be.

Ronald D. Witherup, PSS, STL, PhD
Superior General
Society of the Priests of Saint Sulpice
Paris, 9 October 2019

1 | Understanding the Formation Process

WELCOME TO FORMATION ADVISING. If you are new to seminary and seminary formation, this handbook is written to help you understand the process of seminary formation with a focus on formation advising. Like a person sailing a small boat in a vast ocean where large vessels and land masses suddenly appear, and storms can pop up, a person new to seminary formation will wonder what am I doing and where am I going? This handbook will help you navigate these waters so you survive and thrive in seminary.

This chapter offers you an overview of the formation process by describing the four stages and dimensions of formation, and the major characteristics of the formation. It is Christ who called you into seminary and it is Christ who is the formator guiding you and the entire seminary community through the power of the Holy Spirit. Keeping that in mind, especially during the challenging times in seminary, can be a source of hope and comfort.

The Stages of Priestly Formation

Seminary formation offers you a coordinated process by which you will be trained for priestly life and parish ministry. This process is based on recent magisterial teaching regarding priestly identity and mission.[1] The identity of the priest is found in his conformity to Christ as Head, Shepherd, Servant, and Spouse. His mission is to serve the people of God in the parish by presiding at the liturgy, proclaiming the word, offering the sacraments, leading the people into the mystery of God, and guiding the parish in its participation in the mission of Christ. For a man to develop this identity and fulfill this mission, he needs formation.

The formation process is divided into four stages: (1) A propaedeutic stage, (2) the discipleship stage, (3) the configuration stage, and (4) the pastoral stage. The process of

---

1. This includes St. John Paul II's *Pastores Dabo Vobis* (Washington D.C. Office for Publishing and Promotion Services, United States Catholic Conference, 1992), hereafter, PDV; *The Program of Priestly Formation* (USCCB Publishing: 5th edition. September, 2006), hereafter PPF; the Congregation for the Clergy's recent publication *Ratio Fundamentalis Institutionis Sacerdotalis* (December 8, 2016), hereafter, *Ratio*. Secondly, I have learned a great deal about formation from the approach to formation adopted by the Sulpician Fathers. The Sulpicians, founded by Father Jean-Jacques Olier, are a society of priests whose sole mission is to form men for the priesthood. Finally, I also draw from the field of social psychology and positive psychology and its application to formation particularly as it is presented in executive coaching.

formation is more of a spiral than a straight line. I offer a word about each stage to orient you to the overall approach to formation promoted by the Church.[2]

During the propaedeutic stage, formators provide seminarians with a solid basis for the spiritual life while nurturing self-awareness for personal growth. Seminarians are introduced to the Liturgy of the Hours, make regular use of the sacraments, and become familiar with the Word of God, silence, prayer, and spiritual reading.[3]

Throughout the discipleship stage, formators work to form seminarians into disciples of Christ. All possible effort must go into training a seminarian to walk with Christ, to follow him, and get to know the Lord particularly through the Word.[4] In addition, a great emphasis is placed on human formation during this stage. The holiness of the priest is built upon it and depends on it. As the *Ratio* makes clear, "the importance of human formation cannot be sufficiently emphasized."[5]

During the configuration stage, the focus is on conforming the seminarian to Christ the Shepherd and Servant. This demands that you devote yourself to contemplating the person of Jesus Christ to develop an intimate and personal relationship with the Lord.[6]

The pastoral formation stage occurs throughout the discipleship and configuration stages by gradually introducing

2. *Ratio*, 59–63.

3. *Ratio*, 59.

4. *Ratio*, 62.

5. *Ratio*, 63.

6. *Ratio*, 68.

you to various aspects of ministry with an eye towards ordination and priestly ministry in the parish.[7]

Four Dimensions of Formation

Since the publication of *Pastores Dabo Vobis,* formators have
spoken about the process of formation using the language of
the four "pillars" of formation. The new *Ratio* has replaced
the term "pillars" with the term "dimensions." The image of
"pillars," while helpful for identifying the four features of formation, nevertheless failed to express the integrated relationship among the four dimensions of formation and seemed to
imply that they were external to the seminarian. The language
of "dimensions" holds on to the distinctive nature of each feature of the formation process, while expressing the dynamic
and inherently interdependent and relational nature of the
four features of the formation process. Each dimension of formation interacts simultaneously with the others and aims to
transform the seminarian's heart into the image of the heart
of Christ the Good Shepherd.[8] I will highlight those aspects of
each dimension of formation that the *Ratio* views as important.

Human Dimension

Human formation is the foundation for all priestly formation
since God calls concrete human beings to priestly ministry.[9]

7. *Ratio,* 57.
8. *Ratio,* 89 quoting from *Optatam totius,* 4 and 19.
9. *Ratio,* 63, 94.

By privileging human formation, seminary formation promotes the integral growth of every dimension of the person including physical health, psychological maturity, and
the mature capacity for relationships with men and women.
Human formation fosters emotional maturity, an ability to
be at ease with yourself and others, a sense of responsibility,
creativity and a spirit of initiative. To achieve this kind of
integral growth, you will need to develop self-knowledge
and self-awareness. This occurs as you come to understand
your story, gifts, and weaknesses while learning to integrate
these under the influence of the Holy Spirit. Community
life, ministry, and your relationship with the formators, your
spiritual director, and formation advisor all play a role in
human formation. For those dealing with problematic issues
that stem from their family of origin or other life experiences, psychological counseling will be very beneficial.[10]

Spiritual Dimension

Spiritual formation aims to promote and nourish the seminarian's relationship with God and with all God's people
in friendship with Jesus Christ in the power of the Holy
Spirit. Growing in union with Jesus Christ is a purifying
and transformative experience that is manifest in generous
and sacrificial love. It should inform all your pastoral ministry experiences. Spiritual growth requires participation
in daily Eucharist, praying the Liturgy of the Hours, taking
advantage of the sacrament of Penance, spiritual direction,

---

10. *Ratio*, 94–95.

making an annual retreat, silent prayer, and devotion to Mary and the saints. A special emphasis must be given to chaste celibacy and your relationship to the Word of God.[11]

Intellectual Dimension

Intellectual formation aims to develop the seminarian's knowledge of Scripture and his understanding of theological tradition. Your studies should impact your human, spiritual, and pastoral formation, but more often than not, formation advisors will have to help you make these connections. Theological studies should provide you with the ability to proclaim the Gospel in a way that is credible, captivating, and challenging. At the same time, they should allow you to dialogue with the contemporary world and be able to hear, distinguish, and interpret the many voices in our day in the light of the Gospel. By integrating intellectual formation into the other dimensions of formation, you will develop into a priest who can serve and give witness to the Word in the Church and the world.[12]

Pastoral Dimension

The *Ratio* strongly encourages every dimension of seminary formation to be informed by a pastoral spirit. This dimension of formation challenges every seminarian to learn how to seek out, walk alongside, and lead the people in a spirit

11. *Ratio*, 101–03.
12. *Ratio*, 116–18.

of compassion, generosity, and love. All pastoral ministry courses and all ministry experiences must promote the vision and practice of Christ the Good Shepherd. Pastoral formation involves developing pastoral ministry and leadership skills. It also calls for the development of the art and skill of preaching. In addition, you will need to become an expert in pastoral discernment by listening deeply to the experience of the people, interpreting situations with wisdom, and accompanying the people of God with love.[13]

Four Characteristics of Formation

The formation process that you have entered is marked by four characteristic elements: discipleship, integration, community, and mission.

Discipleship

The process you have embarked on follows the singular journey of discipleship that every Christian undergoes beginning with Baptism and the sacraments of initiation. At the same time, it offers you an intensive form of this journey into discipleship as you come to appreciate how your call to be a disciple of Jesus is at the center of your life and the priesthood. It is a journey into the life of the Triune mystery that occurs through your participation in the seminary community and through the various forms of ministry you take on in seminary.[14]

---

13. *Ratio*, 120.
14. *Ratio*, Introduction, 3.

Integration

Seminary formation fosters the interaction and gradual integration of all four dimensions of formation in the life of the seminarian. A major challenge for you will be trying to keep in balance all four dimensions of formation. There are certain formation experiences that help promote this balance and integration such as community life, hospital ministry, preaching, and leadership opportunities. Your formation advisor and spiritual director can help you reflect on these experiences so you recognize when integration occurs and how valuable it is to priestly life and ministry.[15]

Community

Formation for priesthood is communal in character. In our excessively individualistic culture, this may not be obvious to every seminarian. Yet each seminarian comes from a Christian community to join the seminary community to be sent back to serve the Christian community in his diocese. It is the entire seminary community that participates in your formation. You will be formed by communal liturgy and prayer, and by your relationships with the men in the house, the faculty, and all those you serve. All four dimensions of formation come together and interact most regularly with each other in the communal experiences of formation. It is there that many of the important human formation issues emerge and can be addressed by your formator and spiritual director.[16]

---

15. *Ratio,* 89, 92.
16. *Ratio,* Introduction, 3; also see 90.

Mission

Finally, formation is missionary in character. The Christian community is gathered together by the Spirit to be sent on mission. This missionary impulse belongs to the entire people of God with a special focus on caring for the poor, justice, and peace. This should be reflected in the kinds of ministries selected as part of the pastoral formation program. Seminarians therefore, should be formed as missionary disciples since the goal of all formation is mission.[17] Mission binds together and animates all four dimensions of formation. It is not always obvious to seminarians how human, spiritual, and intellectual formation relate to mission. These topics will need to be discussed in rector's conferences, in spiritual direction, and in formation advising.

Christ: The Formator

Perhaps the most important thing to understand about the process of formation for priestly life and ministry is the role Christ and the Holy Spirit play. In *Pastores Dabo Vobis*, St. John Paul II describes this role:

> "To live in the seminary, which is a school of the Gospel, means to follow Christ as the Apostles did. You are *led by Christ* into the service of God the Father and of all people, under the guidance of the Holy Spirit. Thus you become more like Christ the Good Shepherd in order better to serve the Church and the world as a priest."[18]

17. *Ratio*, Introduction, 3, 91.
18. PDV, 42; emphasis added.

As this passage makes clear, formation for priesthood is a Trinitarian experience. Christ works to form you through the power of the Holy Spirit. The important point to understand is that Jesus Christ is the fundamental formator.[19]

The risen Jesus will use every dimension of seminary life to form you into his image. He acts like a potter shaping you into a disciple and priest who is ready to serve God's people. At times, the Lord will cut things out from your life; at other times, he will introduce new gifts and abilities as he forms and shapes you. The entire seminary experience is designed to support this effort: liturgy, prayer, spiritual direction, philosophy and theology courses, formation advising, life in the house, relationships, and ministry. The potter also uses the formation process to heal, free, reform, and reorient you in the light of the Gospel. Formation, therefore, has a paschal or cruciform character to it. It challenges the seminarian to identify and rid himself of habits, attitudes, assumptions, and behaviors that prevent him from becoming an image of Christ the Shepherd and Servant. It promotes the cultivation of healthy and holy habits that allow Christ to shine through you in a unique way. The good news is that Christ is present to you throughout the formation process. The Lord walks with the you, guides you, and dwells in you every step of the way. At the same time, the Lord walks ahead of you always inviting you to become the person the Lord wants you to become. He is present to you through the community, in his proclaimed Word, in the sacraments, as well as in spiritual

---

19. *Ratio*, 55.

direction, formation advising, and every time you participate in ministry.[20]

Conclusion

Let me conclude this overview by highlighting four important features of the formation process that have emerged from recent magisterial teaching. The first is the conviction that human formation is the foundation of all other dimensions of formation. By emphasizing human formation, the seminary will help you learn about yourself, your life story, your gifts and where you need healing and freedom. By learning about your own self-talk, fears, desires, and hopes, you will become a person who responds rather than reacts to life. Human formation is essential for the spiritual life and pastoral leadership. It will free you to respond to Christ's inspiration rather than your needs and it will prepare you to handle the many challenges that come with leadership in a parish

A second feature of seminary formation that deserves attention is the conviction that the priest is a lifelong disciple of Jesus.[21] Pope Francis reminds us that "formation…is an experience of permanent discipleship, which draws one close to Christ and allows one to be ever more conformed to Him. Therefore, it has no end, for priests never stop being

---

20. *Ratio*, 125.
21. *Ratio*, 54, 62.

disciples of Jesus, they never stop following him."[22] All the baptized are called to live as disciples of Jesus within the life of the Church as she cooperates with the mission of Jesus.[23] The seminarian is a disciple who has discerned a call to live out his discipleship in public ordained service to the people of God. Seminary formation offers an intense training in discipleship where men are formed into visible signs of the merciful love of God the Father.[24]

The third feature worth highlighting is that seminary formation will aid you in the process of becoming conformed to Christ as Head, Shepherd, Servant, and Spouse. This is the work of the Holy Spirit who seeks to transform your heart, mind, and imagination so that you become a unique expression of Christ's presence in the parish. It involves a cruciform process where you will rid yourself of all behaviors, attitudes, and vices that are contrary to Christ while growing in union with Christ so that he is the dominant influence in your life. Conformity to Christ also involves character development and the cultivation of Gospel virtues known as the fruits of the Spirit. The goal of character formation is always other directed—complete giving of yourself in tender love to the people of God.[25]

22.   *Ratio* 54, quoting Pope Francis, *Letter to Participants in the Extraordinary General Assembly of the Italian Episcopal Conference* (November 8, 2014): *L'Osservatore Romano* 258 (November 12, 2014), 7.

23.   *Ratio,* 57.

24.   *Ratio,* 35.

25.   *Ratio,* 36–43.

The final feature of formation follows from the previous one and its implications for the model of leadership a pastor adopts in the parish. There is a close connection between the priest's conformity to Christ the Shepherd and Servant and how the priest relates to and leads the people of God. This relationship is characterized by loving service to God's people as an authoritative leader of the people, teacher of the Word, and minister of the sacraments.[26] By conforming yourself to Christ the Shepherd, you will devote yourself to gathering, accompanying, caring for, and leading his sheep. You will give special attention to the lost sheep.[27] Seminary formation will train you to adopt the model of servant leader who serves with joyful generosity and put the needs of the other ahead of his own. This form of leadership is contrary to the popular forms that emphasize power, control, and prestige. It requires self-awareness and often a real conversion from power to service. You will need to become a man of discernment who lives from a high level of self-knowledge, a deep interior life, and a mature capacity to enter into relationships with others.[28] This form of leadership calls for a transformation that renews your heart and mind so that you can discern what is the will of God. In this way you will be able to choose, decide, and act according to the will of God.[29]

---

26. *Ratio*, 33.
27. *Ratio*, 37.
28. *Ratio*, 41.
29. *Ratio*, 43.

2 | Formation Advising

Two Forms of Accompaniment

Most men find seminary formation to be an intense journey that reorients and transforms their hearts and minds and their sense of themselves. To successfully navigate this process, the seminary provides you with two forms of accompaniment: Communal and personal.[1] Communal accompaniment comes from living with your fellow seminarians and resident faculty. It comes through participation in daily liturgy, communal prayer, various house committees and recreational activities, and the interpersonal relationships, as well as the exchanges and discussions that come with community living.[2] Personal accompaniment comes from your relationship to other seminarians, diocesan brothers, the rector, close friends, your spiritual director, and formation advisor. Both forms of accompaniment are

---

1. *Ratio*, 44–52.
2. *Ratio*, 50–52.

needed throughout the formation process if you are to survive and thrive in seminary.[3]

There is an important difference between spiritual direction and formation advising that is worth highlighting at
this point in our discussion. According to the 1983 *Code of
Canon Law*, spiritual direction in the seminary exists for the
sake of the spiritual formation of candidates for the priesthood. It concerns the spiritual good and spiritual progress of
the seminarian.[4] Traditionally, spiritual direction enjoys the
highest degree of confidentiality such that nothing shared
or uncovered in spiritual direction can ever be revealed to
anyone under any circumstances. In the Sulpician tradition
of seminary formation, the level of confidentiality found in
the internal forum is equated with the seal of Confession.
In practical terms this prevents the spiritual director from
commenting on any of his current or former directees at a
faculty meeting.

Formation advising, on the other hand, operates within
the external forum. It includes discussions you will have with
your formation advisor, the formation faculty, the rector, the
vocation director, and the bishop. It also includes meetings
with vocation directors and seminarians. While formation
advising operates in the external forum, it functions with a
limited confidentiality. What is shared between you and your
advisor is not for public consumption, and often, the advisor does not even share it with other faculty or the vocation

---

3. *Ratio*, 44.

4. *Code of Canon Law* (London: Harper Collins, 1983),
Canons 240, 244, 245, and 246.

director unless the matter is very serious. Yet the assurance of confidentiality in formation advising is limited because your advisor will inform the faculty of your progress when necessary. Nevertheless, some level of confidentiality is necessary to build trust and honest rapport between you and your advisor. This kind of atmosphere is necessary to help you discern your vocation and become aware of your gifts and weaknesses to be more receptive to God's grace.[5]

What is Formation Advising?

Formation advising is the prayerful and reflective practice of accompanying a seminarian through the formation process in the external forum. By accompanying you, your formator seeks to develop a relationship with you so that he comes to know and understand your life story, including your vocation story, interests, desires, and struggles. A formation advisor walks with you as you engage the four dimensions of formation to help you learn about yourself and the ways Christ is trying to form you. He will seek to understand how you are experiencing the various dimensions of formation—what you are learning, what is disturbing you, what is exciting and challenging for you. At times your formator will offer you encouragement, feedback, and the occasional challenge. Through such a relationship, he can help you respond to God's call, understand your experience of formation, and grow into the priest Christ is calling you to become.

---

5. *Ratio*, 46–47.

The approach to formation advising presented here is inspired by the way Jesus formed his disciples. After Jesus called Peter, James, Andrew, and John to follow him, he spent three years forming them into leaders of his mission. He walked with them, ate meals with them, taught them, and regularly invited them to share in his ministry. Sometimes the things Jesus said and did challenged them and even shocked them. Jesus knew these men came to him with their own life experiences and their own assumptions about God and the kingdom. He knew they had developed attitudes and behaviors that needed to be challenged and changed if they were to be his disciples and share in his ministry. Jesus knew each of these men in a personal way. He met them where they were and gave them what they needed at the time it was needed so they could grow into mature disciples. As Jesus walked with his disciples through Galilee or ate meals with them, he listened to them and sought ways to open their eyes to the vision of the kingdom of God that inspired him. He worked to get them to see all God was doing so they could cooperate with the mission of the kingdom. He taught them the prayer of the kingdom. He taught them the virtues of the kingdom. Then he sent them out to share with others what they had learned and who they had become. It was their personal experience of Jesus, their experience of the community of disciples Jesus was forming, the meals they shared with him, and the work they did on behalf of God's coming kingdom that formed them. Their formation reached a new level when Jesus was crucified, rose from the dead, and appeared to them. Filled with the Spirit of God, aware of the presence of the risen Christ, and knowing God's new creation had dawned, they were ready to proclaim the good news, lead the Christian community, and go about the work of Christ.

As we have seen, the formation advisor's chief role is to accompany and guide you through the process of formation. He will walk with you through the joys and struggles of seminary in order to help you learn about yourself and discover how Christ wants to form you each year. As you actively engage the four dimensions of formation, your formator will want to understand how you are experiencing the process, what are you learning, and where you are being challenged. Your formator will also support and promote you as you develop the necessary skills for priestly ministry and as you grow as a disciple of Jesus ready to serve the Church as Christ's shepherd and servant. At times he will mentor you, support and encourage you; at times he will challenge you, coach you, as well as offer insights and observations. Through these different ways of relating to you, he seeks to cooperate with the Lord as he forms you.[6]

The advisor relies on the four dimensions of seminarian formation and the rule of life as a guide as he observes how you are progressing. He regularly observes the following features of the seminarian's life:

- Presence and participation in the common prayer and liturgical life of the seminary;
- Habits of prayer, personal piety, celibate chastity, and simplicity of life;
- A growing clarity about your vocation;

---

6. *PPF*, 80.

- Personal maturity, emotional intelligence, interpersonal skills, social awareness, and leadership abilities;
- A growing understanding of Scripture and theological traditions;
- Mature respect for the Church, the people of God, and pastoral skill develop; and
- The gradual integration of all four dimensions of formation as you grow into your priestly identity and develop the vision and skills for priestly ministry.

Formation Advising Meetings

You will be meeting regularly with your formation advisor. These meetings are not advice sessions or counseling sessions but are conversations structured around your experience of formation, the four dimensions of formation, and the goals you have set with your formator for the year. Your formator will listen to you, ask questions, offer observations and feedback, and occasionally share suggestions for growing in your formation. During the initial meetings, your formator will seek to learn about your life story, your family of origin, and your educational and personal history. He will also want to hear you recount your vocation story and seek to understand where you are with your vocational discernment.

After the initial meetings, discussions will focus on your experience and growth in the four dimensions of formation as you progress through the seminary process. Using the four dimensions of formation as his guide, your formator will be interested in the following topics:

Human Formation

Your formator will want to hear about your experience in your family as you grew up, friendships, educational experience, life history, and vocation story. As you move through the formation process, your advisor will be paying attention to your self-knowledge, emotional intelligence, self-awareness, how you handle conflicts, and your ability to develop relationships. He will also pay attention to your self-image, any perfectionism, self-talk that influences your sense of self, and how past hurts impact how you relate to yourself and others.

Spiritual Formation

Under spiritual formation, he will be paying attention to your attendance and participation at community liturgies. He will discuss your prayer practices, your progress in discerning your vocation, your attitude toward celibacy, and your image of God and the Church. In addition, he will pay attention to how you are growing in your relationship to God and in your awareness of the Holy Spirit alive in your life.

Intellectual Formation

When it comes to intellectual formation, your formator will pay attention to how you are handling the stress of studies, especially during midterms and exams. He may inquire about how you manage stress and discuss ways to improve how you deal with stress by incorporating exercise and socializing into your routine. He will be interested in how you approach studies and how well your study habits are working. Sometimes, you may need help seeing the connection between studies and the other three dimensions of formation. Other times, you may way want to discuss the relationship between your grades and your self-worth.

Pastoral Formation

Throughout your time in formation, your formator will ask about your current experience of pastoral ministry. Important human, spiritual, and pastoral formation issues come up in ministry, especially in hospital ministry and preaching.

Preparing for Formation Advising Meetings

Formation advising meetings take on real depth and meaning when you spend time preparing for these meetings. Life in the seminary is very busy as you move from Mass to class to lunch and many other activities. This makes seminary exciting, but there is a temptation to reduce it to a series of tasks to be completed, thereby missing the deeper dimensions of life where the real formation happens and where the Lord is at work. Pausing to step off this fast-moving train and reflect on your experience does not come naturally, and our American culture, and much of seminary life, does not promote it. If you fail to reflect on your experience since you last met your formator, you will arrive at formation advising with little to say except to report on the tasks you have accomplished and the ones due soon. This makes for superficial and often boring conversation that will compel your advisor to search for something substantial to discuss. But if you spend time prayerfully recalling the main events since you last met your formator, your experience of those events, and, perhaps, where God was in them you will have much to discuss with your advisor. This makes for a rich, powerful, and interesting formation advising meetings in which you get to explore the deeper parts of your experience where real formation occurs and where God is at work. This practice will form you into a man and priest of depth and insight. In our superficial society, the people of God need priests who minister and preach out of an experience of depth in their lives.

Here is how to prepare for your advising meetings:

- Set aside time to prayerfully remember the events since you last met your formator. This may not be easy at first. It may take time to recall some of what you have done during this time. These events will include classes, preparing for tests, writing papers, liturgies, prayer, life in the house, ministry experiences, as well as any family issues that may have occurred. Do not expect to remember all that occurred during that time but allow the Holy Spirit to help you recall some of these events. This may not be easy at first. It may take time to recall what you have done during this time.

- After recalling some of the main events since you last met your formator, go deeper by recalling how you experienced some of these events. How did you react to them? What did these events mean to you in light of the four dimensions of formation? Discovering how you felt during these events, what your motives were, and what they meant to you takes time. This practice will offer you important insights into yourself and how you relate to others. Over time, you will start to notice patterns in your responses to events and in your behavior. You will start to see how the formation issues discussed in advising and spiritual direction are found in your life experience. You will also notice moments of newfound freedom and moments when new virtues and abilities start to emerge.

- Next, seek to find where the Lord was at work in those experiences. This practice will put you in touch with the places where Christ is most active in your life. It will transform your pastoral practices as well.

This kind of practice allows you to process what has been happening to you and helps you recognize the deeper things that are happening in your formation as you rush to complete your many tasks. When you compare the seminarian who engages in this habit with another who does not, the former is dramatically transformed into a priest who loves the Lord and is ready to serve God's people while the latter has barely been touched by the formation process. Regular spiritual direction and formation advising meetings offer you an opportunity to develop this good practice into a habit. The practice of prayerfully reflecting on your experience makes for meaningful advising meetings. It allows you to contribute to and, in part, direct what happens in these meetings.

Your preparation for formation advising should take into account the four dimensions of formation. The following questions can help you focus on each dimension.

- Consider your relationships inside and outside the house: Which were affirming and challenging? Were any strong feelings or memories stirred up? Did your actions and reactions conform with the life of a seminarian?
- Consider your studies: What new insights did you gain and what was challenging?
- Consider your spiritual life: What practices have you used in the past two weeks and have you been faithful to prayer, liturgy and spiritual direction?
- Consider your pastoral ministry if you have one: What went well and what was challenging?

Sharing Your Vocation Story and the Call to Chaste Celibacy

The relationship you develop with your formation advisor will help you to get to know yourself, your vocation, and where and how the Lord is calling you to grow in the formation process. A crucial part of this process will be sharing with your formator your vocation story and how you understand and feel about chaste celibacy. As he listens to your vocation story, he will keep the following questions in mind:

- When did you first consider becoming a priest?
- When and how did that thought or desire begin to emerge for you?

- How did you react to this at first?
- What experiences led you to decide to enter seminary?
- How did your family and friends react to this?
- Why did you decide the diocesan priesthood?
- Where are you now with your discernment regarding priesthood?

Most men who enter seminary are still discerning their call to the priesthood. While discernment can be an internal forum matter, a formation advisor needs to know where you stand regarding your vocation. Most men gradually gain clarity about their vocation during first and second theology. Your formator will check with you at least twice a year regarding your discernment, often at the beginning of the fall semester and after the annual retreat. If you are still discerning your call to the priesthood, your formator can help with this process by discussing with you two approaches to discerning God's will suggested by St. Ignatius of Loyola and described in Father Timothy Gallagher's book *Discerning the Will of God: An Ignatian Guide to Christian Decision Making*.[7]

It will also be important to discuss with your formator your discernment regarding chaste celibacy. Celibacy is a complex topic that touches on all four dimensions of formation. Every seminarian's experience and understanding of celibacy will be shaped by the current cultural attitudes towards celibacy.

---

7.   Timothy Gallagher, *Discerning the Will of God: An Ignatian Guide to Christian Decision Making* (New York: Crossroads Publishing Company, 2009).

It will be helpful to discuss these attitudes with your formator. This is the approach taken by Paul VI in *Sacerdotalis Caelibatus* and the Sulpician Fathers' document on formation for celibacy, *For the Sake of the Kingdom*.[8] Both documents reflect on the positive and negative cultural attitudes regarding celibacy. For instance, today young people value authenticity, generosity, and giving of oneself and these attitudes can support the choice for celibacy. At the same time, we live in a highly "sexualized" consumer culture that struggles with commitment, dismisses the Church as irrelevant, and often considers celibacy as unnatural and even strange.

Formation offers you time to learn about the positive meaning of celibacy by reading Paul VI's encyclical and becoming familiar with the biblical foundations of celibacy.[9] Paul VI's encyclical and the Sulpician document both locate celibacy within the context of the coming kingdom of God, Christ's devotion to the kingdom, and the life of the Church. Set within this context, celibacy is a particular form of discipleship that imitates Christ's gift of self to the kingdom. This imitation of Christ manifests itself as the total self-gift of the celibate to Christ and in service to God's people so that they will grow into the new humanity made

---

8. Paul VI, *Sacerdotalis Caelibatus*, Published June 24, 1967. Accessed at http://w2.vatican.va/content/paul-vi/en /encyclicals.index.html. *For the Sake of the Kingdom: A Sulpician Approach to Formation in Priestly Celibacy* (Paris: Society of the Priests of St. Sulpice, 2005).

9. One study is done by Father Ronald Witherup, PSS, *Seminary Journal* 9, no. 2 (Fall 2003).

possible by Jesus' death and resurrection.[10] Celibacy, then, is
a unique way of relating to Christ and the people of God. It
is relational and mission-oriented in nature. Such a Christ-
centered, kingdom-focused act of self-gift and self-service
will help a seminarian to connect celibacy to human formation, his spiritual life, and his pastoral formation.

Since celibacy is by its very nature relational, human
formation plays an important role in the development of a
healthy and holy celibate life.[11] This cannot be stated enough.
The celibate's renunciation of marriage fosters in the seminarian the capacity to open himself to others in a unique way.
Consequently, all the work that goes into human formation
impacts celibacy. This includes emotional intelligence, the
capacity to relate to others, the ability to listen, and the cultivation of virtues such as self-denial, humility, responsibility,
hospitality, prudence, and availability among others.[12]

You will want to discuss with your formation advisor
how you feel about the sacrifices and struggles that come

---

10. On the relationship between the kingdom of God and
imitating Christ's self-gift, see also Howard P. Bleichner, PSS,
Daniel M. Buechlein, OSB, and Robert F. Leavitt, PSS, *Celibacy for the Kingdom: Theological Reflections and Practical
Perspectives* (Baltimore: St. Mary's 1990, reprinted by Criterion Press, 1997).

11. This is a major theme in *For the Sake of the Kingdom*;
see 11, 14–15, and 18–19.

12. The cultivation of virtues necessary for relating to
others as a celibate is discussed by Paul VI on paragraph 70;
John Paul II in *PDV*, 43; and *For the Sake of the Kingdom,* 18.

with celibacy. You will be giving up having an exclusive intimate partner, marriage, sex, children, and family life. When you begin attending the weddings of your friends, this sacrifice will become real. Those events are often a time when your decision to adopt a celibate life becomes clear. These are experiences to discuss with your formator. There is also the loneliness that comes with celibacy and the stress of non-stop parish ministry. Under the theme of self-knowledge, you will want to consider how you handle stress, pain, and loneliness. What are positive and restorative practices and what are less helpful practices? It will be important for you to learn the signs of when you are getting depleted of energy and the meaning that gives life to ministry. Drinking, overeating, pornography, and overspending are common and addictive ways people cope with stress and loneliness. Then there is "junk food for the soul" such as surfing the web, endless TV watching, and superficial conversations that turn into venting sessions. It will be important for you to identify ways of coping that you have picked up in your life that are helpful and restorative and those habits that are not so healthy or holy. Seminary is a time for you to develop physical, emotional, social, spiritual, and intellectual habits that will help you cope with life's struggles. For diocesan priests, this will always include developing and maintaining relationships with family and friends, with fellow priests, and with the people in the parish.

Spiritual formation is fundamental to living a chaste celibate life. It is important that you discuss with your formation advisor once or twice a year where you stand regarding chaste celibacy. Celibacy is born out of a desire to grow in union with Christ and to abandon oneself to Christ and his kingdom. It is choice made in an effort to grow closer to Christ and to imitate his self-giving life for the sake of the kingdom of God. As George Aschenbrenner suggests, celibacy is a response to Christ's call and to Christ's love. Your spiritual life must be rooted in the attractiveness of God's love. It must be fed by a threefold relationship: with Christ, with fellow priests, and with the people in the parish and in ministry for the people of God.[13]

There are distorted ways to live the celibate life such as the bachelor syndrome, workaholism, clericalism, and private individualism. Be sure to discuss these with your formator so you can develop spiritual practices that prevent your falling into those traps. These will include spiritual direction; personal prayer, especially the examen and *lectio*; retreats; and the cultivation of virtues and friendships. It will also be important to learn the difference between loneliness and solitude. You will face times of loneliness that can be painful. They differ from solitude which is the space needed to hear God's Word and receive God's love so you can share it with the people in powerful ways.

Perhaps the sign that formation for celibacy has taken hold is pastoral charity. "The whole formation imparted to candidates for the priesthood aims at preparing them to enter into communion with the charity of Christ the Good Shepherd."[14]

---

13. George A. Aschenbrenner, SJ, *Quickening the Fire in Our Midst: The Challenge of Diocesan Priestly Spirituality* (Chicago: Loyola Press, 2002), 110–15.

14. *PDV*, 21.

Pastoral charity includes the capacity to love a community and a people, an ability to show warmth and care, and to be available. It will involve relating to women in a positive fashion. Contemplating how Jesus in the Gospels relates to people, especially women, can be a powerful spiritual practice that will feed your capacity to love. The other practice that will teach you to love as Jesus loves is the daily practice of gratitude. That will help you remember how much God loves you and how you are called to love as Christ loves.

Topics for Discussion

Most formation advising meetings will be dictated by what you report about your experience of the previous two weeks. But your formation advisor also has in mind the larger formation process and certain topics that need to be discussed in formation advising. This larger process takes into account where you are during the academic year. During midterms, he will ask about your stress level. During finals, he will ask about your energy level. He will also take into account where you are in the formation process. With new seminarians, he will be checking in on his transition into seminary. With second-year theologians, he will expect to discuss hospital ministry and celibacy. What follows is a list of topics you should expect to discuss according to the four dimensions of formation.

Human Formation

First Year
- Adjustment to the life and routine of the seminary

- Family of origins, life story, and vocation story
- Previous seminary experience
- Trust and openness to the formation process
- Growing self-awareness
- Clear awareness of sexual orientation
- Growth in self-discipline and prudence
- Participating in the life of the community

Second Year
- Ability to manage and/or abstain from addictive substances and addictive behaviors
- Adjusting to clerical life
- Awareness of emotional issues that shape your life
- Developing friendships
- Awareness of celibacy as more than genital deprivation
- Developing the habit of self-care:
  o Healthy bedtime habits: what is your bedtime routine?
  o Exercises: what do you do for exercise?
  o Nutrition: What are you eating and when are you eating?
- Identifying and growing free from perfectionist tendencies
- Feelings regarding hospital ministry

Third Year
- Pastoral year experience with all returning from that experience
- Resolution of major therapeutic needs
- Peaceful acceptance of sexual orientation and needs

- Comfort with solitude
- Acceptance of talents, weaknesses, and limits
- Understanding of the need for exercise and good health
- Growing ability to recognize and understand the emotions of others
- Learning how to handle relationships with friends, family and parishioners
- Emerging spirit of generosity

Fourth Year
- Ability to make sound decisions
- Transitioning out of seminary into full-time priestly ministry
- Awareness of celibacy as a gift
- Ability to remain part of the life in the house while preparing to move on
- Ability to listen to others without judgment
- Approaches to leadership and conflict
- Anticipating emotional support systems after ordination

Spiritual Formation

First Year
- Developing the habit of reflecting on experience and understanding the value of this practice
- Relationship between actions and their moral and spiritual consequences
- Prayer practices and participation in the communal liturgy
- Demonstrates insight into God's call to seminary

Second Year
- Role of Scripture in prayer
- Adjustment to the clerical life
- Understanding and experience of celibacy
- Growing simplicity of life
- Developing a spirit of generosity in the house and in ministry
- Growing free from perfectionism

Third Year
- Clarity regarding and commitment to vocation
- Readiness to pray the Liturgy of the Hours
- Increased integration of spiritual and pastoral life
- Realistic acknowledgement of evil balanced with hope
- Emerging spirit of compassion and mercy

Fourth Year
- Ongoing commitment to spiritual and intellectual formation
- How the diaconate prepares for priesthood
- Ability to see celibacy as a gift
- Integrate obedience and holiness
- Ability to listen to others
- Emerging identity as a leader of the faith community

Intellectual Formation

First Year
- Study habits and adjustment to graduate work in theology

- Impact of social media on study habits
- Developing historical consciousness
- A growing appreciation for the human and divine in the church
- Receptiveness to the ideas and experiences of others

Second Year
- Developing a realistic understanding of the Church as human and divine
- Making connections between theology and ministry

Third Year
- Connections between Scripture, theology and preaching
- Ability to integrate theological concepts into life experience

Fourth Year
- Ecclesiology and parish life

Pastoral Formation

First Year
- Previous ministry experience
- Selecting ministry with the poor
- Reflection on ministry experience

Second Year
- Hospital Ministry
  - Reflections on case studies
  - Reviewing verbatims from hospital ministry

  o Reflection on experience with an eye to human formation issues and pastoral skill development

Third Theology
- Preaching I and II
  - o Experience of preaching
  - o Manner of preparing for homilies
  - o Struggles and areas of growth
  - o Review preaching evaluations
- Parish Ministry I
   Parish ministry experience of the people, staff, and pastor.

Fourth Theology
- Parish Ministry II
   Preaching and sacramental practice in the parish.

3 | Formation as a Process of Growing in Self-Knowledge

THERE IS AN APPROACH TO formation advising that can undermine what God and the Church hope to accomplish through this part of the formation process. This happens when a seminarian takes a superficial approach to formation advising such that the advising meeting is reduced to a check-in or a report on tasks to be completed. This approach misses the deeper realms of experience where the Lord is at work and where real formation occurs. It ignores how much every seminarian has already been formed and deformed by the time he enters seminary. Nor does it consider that real formation and possible transformation occurs on the deep and vast realm of experience that rumbles below the level of daily tasks. This can cause the formator and seminarian to miss where and how the seminarians needs to be healed and freed. They can miss where and how the various dimensions of formation are transforming this man and where and how the Lord is at work in his life.

This chapter invites you to pay attention to the deeper parts of your interior life as you engage formation advising. Drawing on the work of contemporary cognitive psychologists, I set out some key features of the deep and complex internal world you bring to formation. This will mean paying attention to your family history, your desires, imagination, and habits as a way of engaging the deeper realm of experience where real formation occurs.

Where Formation Happens: The Heart and the Imagination

The deeper dimension of a seminarian's life is found in his heart, his deepest desires, and his imagination. It is this deeper dimension of the seminarian's experience where formation occurs. The reason for focusing on the heart, desires, and imagination is that as human beings we are primarily lovers rather than thinkers or doers. We are defined not by what we know, but by what we desire, especially by our deepest desires. Simply put, we are what we love. This understanding of the human person is supported by recent developments in philosophy, neuroscience, and cognitive psychology.[1] By heart, I do not mean merely the place

---

1. James K. A. Smith, *Desiring the Kingdom: Worship, Worldview and Cultural Formation,* Volume 1 (Grand Rapids: Baker Academic, 2009); *Imagining the Kingdom: How Worship Works,* Volume 2 (Baker, 2013); A more popular presentation of this material is found in Smith, *You are What You Love: The Spiritual Power of Habit* (Grand Rapids: Brazos Press, 2016.)

where our feelings originate in the modern romantic sense of the word. A biblical understanding of the heart views it as the center of our consciousness and identity. It is where our deepest desires reside and where our decisions are made. The prophet Ezekiel understood the heart to be the focus of formation when he prophesied that God will take out our hearts of stone and replace them with hearts of flesh and pour his Spirit into us. St. Augustine echoed this view of the human person when he claimed that our hearts are restless until they rest in God. Everyday human experience affirms that we are more feelers than thinkers or believers. We make our way through the day effortlessly without needing to think through each move we make. We wake up, brush our teeth, walk through our house, and drive to work for the most part without thinking about it. When we do this, we are tapping into our unconscious understanding and feeling for things to navigate daily life.[2]

An approach to formation that privileges the heart fits with the *Ratio*'s emphasis on discipleship as the key to formation. When the disciples approached Jesus at the beginning of John's Gospel, he asked them, "What do you want?" (John 1:38). At the end of John's Gospel, he asks Peter, "Do you love me?" (John 21:16). He does not ask them what they know or believe. Discipleship is more a matter of hungering and thirsting than knowing and believing. It is about aligning our loves and desires with Jesus and his kingdom. It is about conforming our will to his will so we desire what God desires. Being a disciple of Jesus calls for a

2. See Smith, *You are What You Love*, 1–25.

pure heart and an imagination shaped by the coming kingdom of God.

Focusing on the heart means paying attention to your
desires. It is our many desires and longings that drive most
of our decisions and actions throughout the day. We are
driven by physical and emotional desires. We are motivated
by a desire for meaning, for truth, power, and respect. These
many desires and longings reside in the heart.[3] Now many
of our desires are trivial like our love for chocolate ice cream
or our desire that the Yankees win the World Series. But
there are deeper, more ultimate desires that orient our life
and shape how we are in the world. These deeper desires
are what fill us with passion and give our lives direction and
meaning. They drive us to "act in certain ways, develop certain relationships, pursue certain goods, and make certain
sacrifices."[4] The former superior general of the Jesuit order,
Father Pedro Arrupe expresses the central role the heart
plays in a person's life:

> Nothing is more practical than finding God,
> than falling in Love in a quite absolute, final way.
> What you are in love with, what seizes your imagination,
>   will affect everything.
> It will decide what will get you out of bed in the morning,
> what you do with your evenings, how you spend your
>   weekends,
> what you read, whom you know, what breaks your heart,

---

3. Smith, *Desiring the Kingdom,* 46–50.
4. Smith, *Desiring the Kingdom*, 52.

and what amazes you with joy and gratitude.

Fall in Love, stay in love, and it will decide everything.[5]

The heart functions as part compass and part engine. As a compass, it directs a person toward the image of the good life and of human flourishing he received from his culture and society. Every person carries this image within his imagination. It expresses what happiness and human flourishing looks like. It shapes our expectations and assumptions about life, particularly what we expect relationships to look like, what counts for work, what flourishing families look like and more.[6] The heart is also like an engine filled with desires that drive us toward this vision of the good life. The attractive and alluring power of this vision captures imagination and evokes in us powerful desires. We are drawn toward it. It directs our desires and decision. It is what we want and crave. This is how we are oriented to the world by what we desire and love.[7]

I mentioned that this image of the good life is carried by our imagination. The imagination is a pre-cognitive faculty by which we navigate and make sense of our world. It is not our ability to be inventive or fantastic—the stuff of make-believe creativity. It functions like an invisible map we unconsciously consult all the time that provides us with an implicit guide for navigating everyday life. It shapes how

---

5. "Fall in Love" Prayer Video, Ignatian Spirituality, accessed October 12, 2019, https://www.ignatianspirituality.com/fall-in-love-prayer-video.

6. Smith, *Desiring the Kingdom*, 52–53.

7. Smith, *Imagining the Kingdom*, 124–26; 137–39.

we perceive and evaluate ourselves, others, and God. Most of us go through life unaware of this orienting map until we find ourselves in a very different culture and suddenly we cannot make sense of things. This can also happen when we meet someone who has a very different vision of the good life than ours. Only then do we realize this map exists.[8] A major task of formation is to help you discover what this assumed image of the good life looks like and how it squares with the kingdom of God.

The everyday rituals and routines that make up the practices of our life are driven by what we love and desire. These daily practices eventually form into dispositions, habits, and perception of the world from which our actions flow. It is important to stress that the loves and desires that orient our life operate most of the time without our thinking about it. They operate like an unconscious desire. They constitute the default orientation we take for granted most of the time. When we follow the invisible map that leads to the good life, we operate from a set of virtues or vices that correspond to the given view of the good life. We develop these habits through various daily practices that make the automatic. These practices form our desires and shape how we love.[9]

Already Formed and Deformed

Long before you entered seminary, you were formed by your family of origin, your educational experience, experience of

8. Smith, *Imagining the Kingdom*, 17–19.
9. Smith, *Imagining the Kingdom,* 157.

church, and our consumer culture. These various people and experiences have promoted a vision of the good life and of human flourishing that is deeply embedded in your imagination. You have unconsciously internalized the values, assumptions, and behaviors of these formative forces by engaging in everyday routines, rituals, and practices such as eating dinner with family, shopping, watching a football game, going to church, texting a friend, or swiping through a dating application. These practices seem innocent enough, but they are very formative. They promote a vision of the good life by telling compelling stories and presenting powerful symbols of the good life. These stories and symbols make powerful, implicit claims about human flourishing and happiness. This is why companies do everything to promote and protect their brands.[10] We tend to surround ourselves with people who share this vision and reinforce our belief in it. As we do so, it seeps into our bones. As it inspires our decisions and actions, it begins to shape our character and identity.[11]

The ways in which a person is formed by family, the nation, Church, and consumer culture would each require

10. Smith, *Desiring the Kingdom*, 75–88. Smith analyzes how the mall, the stadium, and the college campus are very formative of our desires and image of the good life. See also 89–129.

11. Smith, *Desiring the Kingdom*, 54–55. For more on this, see James H. Olthuis, *The Beautiful Risk: A New Psychology of Loving and Being Loved* (Grand Rapids: Zondervan, 2001), 68–70.

a book-length discussion. The emphasis on human formation called for by the new *Ratio* gives due attention to the
ways your family of origin forms and deforms you. Seminary formation should help you to discover and appreciate
the good and healthy ways your family has formed you. It
should also help you identify how it has deformed you and
where you need healing and freedom, often with the help of
a counselor. What is not often taken into account as much
is the powerful ways our nation, our experience of Church,
and our consumer culture play in forming and deforming
us, especially in the light of the Gospel. I will provide a few
words on each to alert you to the ways they form you long
before you arrive at seminary.

Our nation promotes a set of values through the stories it
tells and the symbols and rituals it promotes that causes us
to absorb its vision of the good life. A nationalistic and patri-
otic vision of life is regularly promoted by movies, songs, and
rituals like standing for the national anthem and celebrating
Fourth of July. They contain a story of freedom and national
unity that demands allegiance and loyalty and regularly calls
for sacrifice even to the point of giving one's life for the country. It is important to reflect on this form of formation in the
light of the Gospel and Catholic social teaching.

Your personal religious experience and experience
of Church prior to entering seminary promoted certain
images of God, Jesus, priesthood, ministry, the spiritual life,
and the Church. For most seminarians, these are assumed
images that have not been reflected upon in the light of
Scripture and our rich and varied theological traditions.
As you engage in seminary formation and your theological

studies, these images will be affirmed, challenged, changed, even removed and replaced by others.

It can be argued that consumer culture is the dominant formative force in Western culture. More than anything else, it forms and deforms our desires, our vision of human flourishing, and human happiness. Consumer culture is the water we swim in. We take it for granted without noticing how formative it is.[12] It trains us to value appearance and what a person has achieved, especially through financial gain and power. It is the rich, beautiful, and famous who are revered in this culture. These people, we are told, have friends, joy, and love. This is the kind of life we are trained to desire. There is a sharp contrast between the glamorous vision of the good life found in advertisements, sit-coms, and movies and our daily life. The people in those advertisements and movies have what I do not have but want. Since I do not have what they have something must be missing and wrong with me. If I just buy this product, I will be whole and happy. But my lack of satisfaction and happiness re-emerges not long after the product is purchased. Consumer culture also fosters competition among friends and colleagues. Since we are valued by our appearance and not our character, we are in an endless competition for appearing a certain way dictated

---

12.   Two important books on this subject are: William T. Cavanaugh, *Being Consumed: Economics and Christian Desire* (Grand Rapids: Eerdmans Publishing, 2008) and Vincent T. Miller, *Consuming Religion: Christian Faith and Practice in a Consumer Culture* (New York: Continuum Publishing, 2004).

by the whims of the current fashion trends. This competition reduces everyone to an object either of attraction or revulsion. Girls and women are objectified as bodies to be desired according to a certain standard.[13] Consumer culture, especially in the United States, plays a major role in the presence of racism and sexism in our society by reducing all things, especially African Americans, women, and girls to a commodity to be sold or scapegoated for our country's ills.[14]

How can we be saved from our constant failure to match up, from the endless competition, and from the wound that comes by being objectified? Consumer culture offers us an answer, making it, therefore, the problem and the solution. Shopping is construed as a kind of healing therapy that can help a person deal with the sadness and frustration of our broken world. The thrill of the purchase and the sheen of the new and novel are supposed to offer us the happiness, pleasure, and fulfillment we long for. It is a world of constant consumption that plays on our desire for more by offering us the next new thing. Consumer culture promises that every desire you have can be fulfilled right now with a click of a mouse or swipe of your finger. No waiting, no putting off, no self-restraint is necessary.[15]

---

13.   For an eye-opening account of how this happens, see Sharon Lamb Packing, *Girlhood: Rescuing Our Daughters from Marketers' Schemes* (New York: St. Martins, 2006).

14.   For a well-documented indictment of the collusion between U.S. economic institutions with slavery, see Edward E. Baptist, *The Half Has Never Been Told: Slavery and the Making of American Capitalism* (New York: Basic Books, 2016).

15.   Miller, *Consuming Religion*.

Seminary formation invites you to discover the ways you have been formed and deformed by these powerful forces. What makes this so challenging is that we spontaneously internalize many of the values and beliefs promoted by our nation, Church, and consumer culture. They influence what we love, desire, and imagine as the good life. Cognitive psychologists tell us that the vision of the good life these values promote and the desires that drive us operate in the unconscious. They influence how we live without our knowing it.

The Deep World Within

For further insight into how you are influenced by the vast world of the unconscious and its significance for formation, you need to learn about the two different systems that work together in your brain all the time. One system is visible and easily recognizable and the other is hidden most of the time. The visible system is associated with your conscious activities. These are mental acts we are aware of, that require effort, and over which we have control, such as doing our taxes. The hidden system is traditionally called the unconscious or the adaptive unconscious. It operates quickly and automatically, while the visible system is slow and deliberate. The visible system is at work when we are reading directions, working on a math problem, or learning a new language or piece of music. The hidden system of the unconscious is at work when we respond with fear to a scary movie or when we ride a bicycle or drive a car effortlessly. The unconscious contains our habits and all the skills we have learned allowing us to respond and act quickly without thinking, especially in dangerous situations. It is a vast hidden world that operates underneath our consciousness. Our conscious and unconscious mental processes do different things. Both are at work all the time and can support and cooperate with each other.[16]

When you arrive at seminary and begin formation, you carry with you your life history and a deep, vast world you depend on all the time but pay little to it. By sharing with you some of the recent research on the hidden unconscious system at work in your life, the hope is that you will appreciate the deep and wide mystery and history you bring to formation. This research shows that most of your everyday life is determined by mental processes put into motion by our environment that operate outside of conscious awareness. This vast, hidden, and complex world lies hidden in your unconscious and has a powerful influence over your conscious actions.[17] For three decades, Professor John Bargh of Yale University has been studying this world and its relationship to conscious thought and behavior.[18] He has identified three dimensions of this world: the hidden past, the hidden

---

16.   Daniel Kahneman, *Thinking, Fast and Slow* (New York: Farrar, Straus and Giroux, 2011), 19–24; Timothy Wilson, *Strangers to Ourselves: Discovering the Adaptive Unconscious* (Cambridge, MA: Belknap Press, 2002).

17.   John A. Bargh and Tanya L. Chartrand, "The Unbearable Automaticity of Being," *American Psychologist* 54, no. 7 (July 1999): 462–79.

18.   John Bargh, *Before You Know It* (New York: Touchstone, 2017).

present, and the hidden future. The relationship between this hidden world and our conscious self can be expressed by the image of a small island surrounded by a vast ocean. The island with its the plants, trees, and animals represent our conscious self. The ocean surrounding the island with its hidden world teeming with life that only rarely comes to the surface represents our unconscious self. Another image for this relationship is that of a computer screen with its visible icons and a vast network of unseen software running in the background making it all work. The icons, images, and text we see on our computer represent the conscious visible dimension of our brain, while the many software programs making the computer operate represent the complex activities happening in the unconscious hidden system of our brain. Growing in self-knowledge is a major goal in seminary formation. Understanding the various dimensions of our hidden world will help you appreciate the importance of this goal and know what to look for in your experience and share with your formator.

The Hidden Past

Every person carries within his unconscious the long-hidden past. This includes his ancient evolutionary history, forgotten childhood, and the culture he grew up in. Our ancient ancestors lived in a world that was often far more dangerous than ours. We inherited from them the unconscious drive for physical safety and survival. We are born with two survival skills that operate from the unconscious. The first is the automatic reflex that helps us deal with the many-sided dangers of the world. This lightning-quick system recognizes threats to our safety and survival by generating involuntary emotions such as fear and worry. It also releases the hormone adrenaline so we can either fight or flee. Secondly, survival in that dangerous world depended on our ancestors cooperating with those they trusted and being able to coordinate activities with them. Fear, worry, and cooperation were essential for survival since they needed to run from those who appeared menacing and work with those who seemed trustworthy. We come equipped with the ability to quickly evaluate who can be trusted and the ability to read the emotions of others.[19]

Another part of our hidden past comes from childhood. Every child is born with the capacity to bond with parents and family. Even though most people have no memory of what happened to them before the age of five, those experiences are retained in our implicit memory that is housed in hidden system of the unconscious. They have an enormous impact on our capacity to trust others and develop friendships. A person develops a secure or insecure attachment depending on how his main caregivers related to him and met or failed to meet his needs at this early age. Researchers have found that those who experienced social warmth as infants had an innate tendency to develop social warmth and trust toward others. Those with an insecure attachment from a lack of social warmth as infants, struggle to develop relationships and to trust others. A person with an insecure attachment can develop a secure attachment later in life. The point is that

19. Bargh, *Before You Know It*, 35–51.

these experiences shape our assumptions about the world, our feelings towards others, and confidence in ourselves.[20]

Infants learn the language, culture, and ideology of the country they are raised in. The cultural assumptions absorbed during childhood permeate our lives. Culture is like water to fish. We swim in it, take it in, and hardly notice it. Consequently, the unconscious learning every child engages in plays an important role in character formation. Researchers have shown that children are like sponges who soak up the environment they are raised in. They take in and internalize all the explicit and implicit values, preferences, and assumptions expressed by family and their caregivers.[21] Much to the surprise of researchers, stereotypes and prejudice are embedded even before kids start school, especially when it comes to race, gender, and faith.[22] These long-learned values, assumptions, and prejudices are the kinds of things seminary formation seeks to expose, and when contrary to the Gospel, free a person from.

The Hidden Present

In recent years, psychologists and neuroscientists have discovered that our unconscious performs many operations that make much of everyday life possible. This is the hidden

20. Bargh, *Before You Know It*, 56–67.

21. Bargh, *Before You Know It*, 72.

22. Bargh, *Before You Know It*, 85–92. See Michelle Alexander's discussion of implicit racism in *The New Jim Crow* (New York: The New Press, 2010), 103–06.

present of our unconscious mind. It functions like a vast underground world of hidden software programs operating constantly. For instance, there is a program that makes us aware of where our body is at all times. Another ensures that our motor skills are running. There is a language program that works instantly with memory to store and retrieve words, expressions, and their meaning for speaking, reading, and writing. There is a filtering program that helps us sort through the 10,000,000 pieces of information our five senses take in at any given moment.[23]

Researchers have found that our unconscious mind is constantly working 24 hours a day. Known as the Unconscious Thought Theory (UTT), researchers have found that the mind is working around the clock making judgments and decisions. For instance, our unconscious mind is constantly evaluating people and situations as good or bad, deciding if we like or dislike someone or some situation. This explains how we can have immediate reactions to people and experiences such as food, sunsets, and other people without thinking about them. These unconscious and automatic reactions and evaluations signal to us whether we should stay or go, approach or avoid a person or situation.[24] At the same time, our minds are constantly working on problems we need to solve and goals we want to achieve. The part of the brain that was active when consciously learning remains active when our conscious mind becomes distracted or works on something else.[25]

23. Wilson, *Strangers to Ourselves,* 19–24.

24. Bargh, *Before You Know It,* 126–37.

25. Bargh, *Before You Know It,* 160.

There is another dimension of this research that is crucial to the work of formation. Researchers John Bargh and Tanya Chartrand point out that so much of what we learn happens implicitly and unintentionally.[26] From birth, we are immersed in all sorts of environments beginning with our families, schools, sports teams, neighborhoods, and work places. We are primed to unintentionally internalize attitudes and assumptions from those environments. This is how children learn their native language without studying it. It is how children learn they are loved. Through this process of unintentional learning, we develop implicit views of ourselves. It is how we develop our value system, how we perceive the world, and internalize stereotypes. A large part of formation involves identifying the values and assumptions you have learned from our culture and where they stand in the face of the values of the kingdom of God.

The unconscious plays an important role in how we learn and develop skills of all sorts. Any person who learned to play the violin, drive a car, or speak another language knows how difficult any of these activities can be at first. However, with regular practice and coaching they can become easy and automatic. As these skills become automatic, conscious choice drops out.[27] Neuroscientists tell us how this happens. When we try a new skill, fresh neural networks are created. With practice, these neural networks grow a fatty tissue called myelin to insulate the nerve fibers increasing

---

26. Bargh and Chartrand, "The Unbearable Automaticity of Being."

27. Kahneman, *Thinking, Fast and Slow*, 19–24.

the speed, strength, and accuracy of the signal. As this happens, the skill or habit becomes automatic. After a certain amount of practice, the brain moves knowledge and skills we learn and develop from the conscious level to the vast storehouse of our unconscious. The brain constantly moves explicit knowledge, skills, and habits into our unconscious so that we can draw on them automatically. This saves the brain enormous amounts of energy. Musicians, athletes, and anyone learning a new feature on their computer, go through this process. Seminarians experience this when they learn to preach and learn how to lead a liturgical event. At first it can be quite taxing, but eventually much of it can be done automatically. Knowing about how the mind moves knowledge and skills acquired from the conscious to the unconscious mind, from a difficult practice to an automatic one can be a source of great motivation for seminarians learning new skills.[28]

The Hidden Future

Researchers have also found that our mind is constantly working on our future. When nothing else is going on, our mind enjoys working on problems yet to be solved and on goals yet to be realized. This is the role the hidden future plays in our unconscious mind.[29] There are two ways the

---

28.   For a helpful discussion of the role myelin plays in the formation of habits good and bad see Daniel Coyle, *The Talent Code: Greatness Isn't Born, It's Grown. Here's How* (New York: Bantam Books, 2009), 30–46.

29.   Bargh, *Before You Know It*, 238.

unconscious mind is oriented towards the future. The first involves future goals and desires each of us has. Who and what we want to be in the future shapes what we think, feel, and do in the present. We see the world through goal-colored glasses.[30] Often our goals and long-term desires motivate us in unconscious and hidden ways while influencing much of what we do. For instance, we are driven to survive, to mate, to eat, be safe, to belong, and socialize. When these goals are triggered by external influences, they can redirect what we pay attention to and even what we remember. They can even cause us to override many of our most cherished values and moral beliefs. It is important that you identify the deeper goals and motivations that can drive your behavior.[31]

The second way our unconscious mind is oriented toward the future involves problems that need to be solved. Behind the scenes, our mind is constantly working on our future—problems to be solved, goals to be achieved, insights to be discovered. Various researchers have proposed different kinds of problems and puzzles to demonstrate just how good the unconscious is at solving problems. Many scientists, artists, and intellectuals have come to a new insight or solved a problem while doing or thinking about something else or while simply dreaming. This gives evidence for the advice of sleeping on it. It provides a reason for starting papers, homilies, and other projects ahead of time so the unconscious mind can work on them.[32]

---

30. Bargh, *Before You Know It*, 214.

31. Bargh, *Before You Know It*, 214–29.

32. Bargh, *Before You Know It*, 239–56.

I have been discussing the many dimensions of the hidden world that you bring to formation advising. This hidden world contains deep influences from the past, present, and future that shape your behavior, choices, likes, and dislikes. Most of us are unaware of these influences and activities that are constantly at work in our hidden self. The hope is that you now have a greater appreciation of the mysterious hidden world you bring to the formation process.

It should be clear how much of your vision of the good life with its attendant desires, values, and habits resides in the unconscious. A large part of formation involves discovering this hidden, assumed world that influences how you live and react to life. As you discover some of these deep desires, dispositions, and values, you will need to reflect on them in the light of the Gospel to discern which of them are distorted and deformed and need to be abandoned, and what is true and good and needs to be further developed. The good news is that the vision of the good life promoted by the gospel with its values and attitudes has also been internalized by a person entering the seminary. The entire seminary process offers him an intense course in this Gospel vision with practices such as communal and personal prayer, spiritual direction, formation advising, studies, and ministry to help you internalize the Gospel vision of life and human flourishing.

Implications for Formation

Let me summarize what we have been discussing in this chapter by highlighting the implications it has for your experience of formation. It should be clear by now that you enter seminary already formed by your family of origin, the values of our nation, and our consumer culture. The ways in which your desires, imagination, view of the good life, and things that you love have all been influenced by these sources. At the same time, you have been formed by the Church and your faith journey. Both forms of formation influence you and operate from the hidden world of the unconscious that emerges in your reactions, feelings, interests, decisions and actions. Much of seminary formation involves growing in self-knowledge regarding the ways you have been formed.

Since you have already internalized the ways your family, our nation, and consumer culture have formed you, it is easy to take much of that for granted. But you probably have some sense of how they view relationships and the good life is often contrary to the vision of human flourishing and happiness found in the kingdom of God as proclaimed and embodied by Jesus. Much of the formation received from one's family and our consumer culture is actually a defor- mation and a distortion of desires, values, and actions seen in the light of the kingdom of God. Consequently, you carry within you rival stories about the good life and contending visions of human flourishing. You will have contrary desires and longings struggling for dominance and attention along with contending dispositions and habits. These two visions of the good life produce contrary perceptions of the world. On the one hand, you have been trained to believe you are the center of all things, while the Church claims Christ is the center of the universe. Consumer culture has trained you in the practice of instant gratification and self-promotion, while the Gospel calls for self-denial and concern for the needs of the other. When the light of Gospel and the kingdom of God is shone on your previous formation, you will start to notice how distorted that vision of the good life and human flourishing can be.

You also arrive at seminary already formed by your prior experience of Church and your faith journey. This has shaped your image of God, Christ, the world, the Church, faith, ministry and many other dimensions of the Christian life. Much of this conforms to the Gospel and the kingdom of God proclaimed and embodied by Jesus Christ and the traditions of the Church. Nevertheless, this formation can be a limited and often partially distorted view of the Christian life. You must expect the process of seminary formation to be, at times, challenging and even disorienting at first. A part of that challenge will come from theological studies, from ministry, discussion with other seminarians, retreats, and the many other experiences of seminary life. Part of you will resist thinking in new ways while another part of you will be open to it. Formation advising and spiritual direction offer you a place to discuss these experiences and negotiate the conflict between your assumed view of the faith and that presented by the various dimensions of seminary formation.

Seminary formation offers you an intense embodied experience of the kingdom of God as proclaimed and embodied by Jesus Christ. All four dimensions of formation should promote an experience of the risen Jesus and the Spirit so that you will internalize the vision of the good life and human flourishing shaped by the coming of the kingdom of God and the dawning of God's new creation.[33] This is the kingdom of God proclaimed by Jesus in the Gospels, by Paul in his letters, and embodied by the crucified and risen Jesus. As you experience the kingdom coming into your life through Christ and the Spirit and internalize the story of the kingdom, a new view of yourself and your relationships will emerge. Your entire spiritual life, particularly liturgical, communal prayer, as well as personal prayer and retreats will offer you experiences of the kingdom coming into your life. Your studies should correct and clarify distorted views of the kingdom of God. You will need to immerse yourself in the story of the Gospel as expressed by communal and personal practices and rituals beginning with liturgy and communal prayer as well as community life, formation meetings, retreats, and ministry. Meanwhile, your use of pastoral skills in ministry will gradually be informed and inspired by your experience of the kingdom and your growing vision of the kingdom of God.

Formation for the Christian discipleship and the priesthood involves the conversion of the imagination, the purifying and redirecting of your desires, and the sanctifying of your perception through the development of a new vision of self, others, God, the Church, Christian ministry, and

---

33.   For more on this subject see, N. T. Wright, *Surprised by Hope: Rethinking Heaven, the Resurrection and the Mission of the Church* (New York: HarperOne Publishing, 2008); *Simply Good News: Why the Gospel is News and What Makes It Good* (New York: HarperOne Publishing, 2014); *Surprised by Scripture* (New York: HarperOne Publishing, 2015)

creation. Unlearning of old habits and attitudes will be part of this process. Discovering the vision of God's new creation coming through Jesus' resurrection and what it means for discipleship and priestly ministry is the other part. In short, seminary formation involves the reorientation and transformation of your imagination and desires and the sanctification of your perception of things so you learn to act in the service of the kingdom of God.[34]

34. In Smith, *Imagining the Kingdom*, chapter four offers a discussion of how liturgy can reorient the imagination and sanctify our perception.

4 | The Power of Participation

Both St. John Paul II in *Pastores Dabo Vobis* and Pope Francis in the new *Ratio* call on seminarians to be actively engaged in their formation. Both John Paul II and Francis know that the more you take an active role in your formation, the more it can transform you into a holy and healthy priest. Taking responsibility for your own growth and development in all four areas of formation is essential for every parish priest. There is a deeper reason behind its impact on priestly life and ministry. When you actively engaged in the formation process, you are cooperating with the risen Lord who called you to this life and is the Formator. Realizing that the Lord seeks to form you into a disciple and transform you into his image will prevent you from adopting a passive approach to formation or to view it as a matter of completing tasks. Instead, you will see it as an experience of discovery, of growing in freedom, and self-knowledge. It will be a journey into discipleship with Christ and how he wants you to serve God's people. Knowing that Christ wants to transform you into a priest who reflects Himself the Good Shepherd and Servant will give you motivation when seminary can be frustrating and hard work. This chapter suggests various ways you can participate fully in the formation process.

Fostering a Growth Mindset

When you take an active role in your formation, you start to develop what psychologist Carol Dweck calls a "growth mindset."[1] In her research into what motivates people to act, Dweck discovered two different ways people are motivated. The first group maintains a "fixed mindset." People with this mindset, whether they be students, athletes or employees, are motivated by a desire to receive recognition and approval. They are not motivated by a desire to grow and improve for its own sake. Dweck and her colleagues found that this group is less likely to take risks and try something new. They are afraid if they fail, they will not receive the recognition they want. Failure was devastating for them. This approach undermines their ability to grow beyond their original promise.

The second group, Dweck found, lives from a "growth mindset." This group is motivated by the desire to improve. They are open to taking risks. Failure for them offers insight into areas they need to improve on. This is the mindset of the lifelong learner. It is the mindset that makes for a transformative experience of formation. The seminarian who takes charge of his formation will more than likely have a growth mindset. But it is quite easy for a seminarian to work for recognition rather than personal growth.

---

1. Carol Dweck, *Mindset: The New Psychology of Success* (New York: Ballantine Books, 2008).

Three concrete approaches to formation advising follow from Dweck's research. First, you will benefit from discussing with your formator these two different mindsets. Most people live from one or the other without thinking about it. If you come to seminary with a growth mindset, you should be encouraged to continue with this approach. If you discover you have been formed into a fixed mindset, you will need help identifying when you approach experiences with this mindset. You will need to work at adopting a growth mindset with the help of your formator and spiritual director.

Secondly, explore what motivates your approach to study, grades, and performance in preaching and ministry. This is often the quickest way to uncover which mindset motivates you. There are important human and spiritual formation issues that can be explored here. Beneath the question of motivation is the question of identity and self-worth. To what extent have you heard the good news that you are loved by God and that your self-worth and identity are not tied to performance? To what extent are you seeking self-worth through performance and recognition from others? How and where do you find meaning? These are important formation issues to explore along these lines.

Thirdly, you will want to work with a formation advisor who understands and supports a growth mindset. The formator who does this will praise and encourage effort rather than results. Instead of praising you for a great homily, he will praise the work you put into developing and delivering your homily. Some formators may not know about Dweck's work. You can introduce a formator to it and request that formation advising be done from that point of view. As mentioned above, this approach will support your engagement in the formation process. It will encourage you to seek ways to grow and improve. Formation advising becomes a partnership in which you find support, encouragement, and guidance from your formator. It will foster an atmosphere where it is safe to ask questions such as where can I improve? What can I learn from this? What can I change?

The value of this approach can be seen when we consider how it impacts the approach you take to human formation and preaching. Instead of being driven by the fear of a formator finding your weaknesses, you will view formation as a chance to learn about yourself, to grow in freedom, to find healing and wholeness. A preacher who impacts the people of God must be a lifelong learner who constantly studies the Bible and the lives of the people. Adopting a growth mindset will allow you to grow, change, try new things as a preacher, and accept criticism in order to improve all aspects of your preaching. You will continually ask questions such as: how can I improve my preparation process, what are new ways I can organize my homilies to better deliver my message, what are the best Protestant and Catholic preachers doing, how can I improve my delivery, and how can I better connect with the people?

The Practice of Regular Reflection

As you develop a growth mindset, you will also cultivate the habit of regularly reflecting on your life experience. [2] This

---

2. *Ratio*, 58: "The seminarian is required to…review his own life constantly."

wide-ranging practice will help you grow in self-knowledge. Regular meetings with a spiritual director, formation advisor, and a ministry supervisor offer you opportunities to develop this habit. We live in a culture that drives us to focus on the next new thing and the next task to be done. Our culture does not train us to pause and reflect on our experience. But for you to move beyond a superficial task-oriented way of living, you must develop the prayerful practice of reflecting on all four dimensions of formation. This practice will help you make sense of your life, see the deeper movements in your life, face up to some of the distorted behaviors that are part of your story, while recognizing the ways God has been at work in your life and is at work each day.

The practice of regular reflection can be applied to each of the dimensions of formation. For instance, to take an active role in human formation you will need to reflect on your relationships past and present, on your emotional reactions in various situations, and on how well your way of relating to others is informed by the Gospel or not. This also includes reflection on your health, diet, and exercise. Intellectual formation requires you to reflect on how you handle the stress of studies, what is your attitude towards theological studies, and whether they impact how you envision the spiritual life and ministry. Spiritual formation calls for regular reflection on your relationship to God, your prayer practices, how well you cooperate with the Lord, and how much you are embodying the Gospel in your relationships. Pastoral formation calls for regular reflection on pastoral practice: how well do you listen, how often do you respond to God's people, and how well you preach the Gospel and lead the people in liturgical events? This kind of regular reflection will make for rich discussions in spiritual direction and formation advising.

The following questions can help you reflect on your experience:

- Consider your relationships inside and outside the seminary house: Which were affirming and challenging? Were any strong feelings or memories stirred up? Did your actions and reactions conform with the life of a seminarian?
- Consider your studies: What new insights did you gain and what was challenging? How do you feel about your studies?
- Consider your spiritual life: What practices have you used in the past two weeks and have you been faithful to prayer, liturgy, and spiritual direction? Over the past two weeks, what has your relationship with God been like?
- Consider your pastoral ministry: What went well and what was challenging?

Formation Goal-Setting Process

Another way you can take charge of your formation is by engaging in an annual goal setting process early in the fall semester.[3] Formation works well when you set clearly defined, concrete goals that fit with where you have been

---

3. This journaling process is based on material Fr. David Thayer, PSS, shared with me.

and where you are going in formation. The following goal setting process can help you identify meaningful goals for the year. This process takes into account what is happening right now in your life, the ways you have changed and grown in seminary, and where you are being called to grow in terms of the four areas of formation.

This process is a prayer practice meant to be done under the guidance of the Holy Spirit. Begin by lighting a candle, reverencing Scripture, and spend some time quieting down. You can do this by noticing your breath for a few seconds and conducting a slow scan of your body noticing how different parts of your body feels from your feet to the crown of your head. After quieting down, spend a moment realizing you are in God's presence. Then ask the Holy Spirit to assist you in prayerfully considering where you are and where you are going.

Step 1. Where am I?

The first part of the process involves reviewing your experience since arriving this year in seminary. Recall the major events you have experienced thus far this year. As you recall these events, pay attention to the various feelings that came up from when you arrived at seminary up until the current moment. Were you anxious about arriving for the first time? Glad or sad to settle in? What feelings did you have after his first classes of the semester?

Then ask the Holy Spirit to help you recognize where the Lord was present to you thus far -in the words of a friend, in a group experience, a sermon, conference, wherever?

Jot down in your journal the images, insights, events and feelings that came to mind as you review your experience of seminary this year. Then review what you wrote down. Is there anything you wished to add? Is there a common theme?

Conclude step one by giving thanks for all the good you have received thus far this year and for the ways God has been present throughout all these events.

Step 2. Who am I?

After reviewing what happened since arriving at seminary, go deeper with this reflection by asking the Holy Spirit to help you consider how wonderfully God has made you. Consider the gifts you are aware of this time in your life including family, friends, education, and life experiences. Also consider personal gifts God has given you. Perhaps you are a good listener, or a good student, or perhaps you are kind and generous. Note of these gifts in your journal while giving thanks to God.

Next, ask the Holy Spirit for insight into where the Lord is asking you to grow and change. Perhaps you need to work your relationship skills or managing stress or maybe you need to develop new skills for ministry. Jot down in your journal these insights. Also ask the Holy Spirit for help in overcoming any obstacle that prevents you from becoming the person Christ wants you to be.

Step 3. Where am I going?

After considering what is happening in your life and how much God has given to you, formulate one concrete

THE POWER OF PARTICIPATION 69

achievable goal you want to accomplish this year in each of the areas of human, intellectual, spiritual and pastoral formation. Write down one goal for each dimension of formation and discuss these with your formator.

Human Formation

Human formation aims to develop in a seminarian the mature capacity to relate to men and women of different ages and social situations. Reflect on the following dimensions of human formation to develop at least one concrete goal and strategy for achieving that goal this year:

- Self-knowledge
- Self-awareness
- Social-awareness
- Knowledge of family of origins
- Knows his strengths and weaknesses
- Physical health and exercise
- Affective maturity
- Capacity for relationships
- Handling stress
- Conflict management
- Takes initiative and responsibility
- Leadership

Spiritual Formation

Spiritual formation aims to promote and nourish a seminarian's communion with God in friendship with Jesus in the power of the Spirit. Reflect on the following features of spiritual formation and select at least one concrete goal and strategy to focus on this year.

- Vocational discernment
- Growing in his relationship with the Lord
- Participation in daily Eucharist
- Faithfully praying the Liturgy of the Hours
- Understanding and practicing chaste celibacy
- Developing a set of personal prayer practices, especially *Lectio Divina*
- Participating in the sacrament of reconciliation and receiving spiritual direction
- Cultivating virtues such as a welcoming spirit, patience, humility and compassion.

Intellectual Formation

Intellectual formation aims to achieve in the seminarian a solid understanding of philosophy and theology to allow him to proclaim the Gospel to people in a way that is accessible and credible. Reflect on the following characteristics of intellectual formation and select at least one concrete goal and strategy for the year.

- An ability to learn for its own sake and for the sake of ministry
- A desire to understand the meaning of our faith
- Keep up with readings and plan and complete assignments on time.

- Integrate theological studies into his spiritual life and pastoral ministry
- Developing the habit of ongoing learning
- Cultivate a knowledge of our culture and current events
- Reflect critically and creatively on his experience and our society in the light of the Gospel
- Develop a knowledge and love for God's Word.

Pastoral Formation

Pastoral formation aims to form priests into the image of Christ the Good Shepherd whose ministry is marked by compassion, generosity and love for all. Reflect on the following characteristics of pastoral formation and select at least one concrete goal and strategy for the year.

- Develop the capacity to relate to others in a mature way that is engaging while respecting boundaries.
- Pastoral skills such as listening, flexibility, planning, cooperation
- Cultivate a love for God's People, especially the poor
- Emphasize the Word of God in teaching and preaching
- Developing the skills for preaching that includes discovering the message, crafting the homily to express the message and delivering the message
- Develop the skill of pastoral discernment and good judgment
- Learns how to accompany the people of God by seeking them out, promoting their charisms, walking with them and leading them into the Triune Mystery

- Cultivating the ability to dialogue with people.
- Possesses a desire to serve God's People and a missionary spirit to go where the Bishop needs him to go.

Conclusion and Follow-Up

After giving thanks to God for this exercise, email a copy of your goals to your formation advisor so he can discuss them with you in the next meeting.

Growing in Emotional Intelligence

An important indication that you are engaged in the formation advising process is your growth in self-knowledge. This can happen in a number of ways. The regular practice of preparing for formation advising meetings and the discussions that follow are an important way you can grow in self-knowledge. The same is true for when you recount your life story and vocation story. Another is by reflecting on pastoral ministry and the composition of the end-of-year evaluation. Another valuable way to grow in self-knowledge regarding your relationship with yourself and others is by reading and discussing the book *Emotional Intelligence 2.0*[4] with your formator.

Cultivating the Capacity for Relationships

As mentioned above, the goal of human formation is the development of a mature capacity for relations with men and

---

4.   Travis Bradberry and Jean Greaves, *Emotional Intelligence 2.0* (San Diego: TalentSmart, 2009).

women of various ages and social conditions.[5] The process of developing such a capacity is long and complex. It involves your growing in maturity, self-knowledge, self-confidence, and inner freedom. Your relationship with the men in the seminary house, your formator and spiritual director, and the people you encounter in ministry will be the situations where this capacity to relate to others emerges. A formator can play an important role in this process by offering you feedback about the way you relate to others, and suggestions for how to relate to others. If you come from a home where healthy relationships were the norm and where you received a secure attachment, this process began very early in life. If you grew up in difficult home situation that did not provide a secure attachment, this process may not begin until seminary.

Developing the capacity to relate to others in a mature way depends on the development of three skills: self-awareness, self-management, and social awareness. These skills are regularly associated with emotional intelligence.[6] Self-awareness refers to your capacity to perceive your own emotions in the moment and to understand how you tend to react emotionally in various situations over time. It requires the skill of self-management where you use your awareness of your emotions to be flexible in social situations by directing your behavior in ways appropriate to the current situation. This requires impulse control and the personal freedom to put your needs on hold and to manage your personal tendencies

---

5. *Ratio*, 95.

6. This material is based on Bradberry and Greaves, *Emotional Intelligence 2.0*.

so to be in service of the other. Social awareness refers to the ability to pick up on the emotions of others. The more you are aware of your own emotions, the more you will be able to perceive what other people are thinking and feeling. This calls for further maturity and freedom because it requires you to stop talking and stop the monologue in your head to listen to and observe others.[7]

The following are strategies you can practice to develop the three skills of emotional intelligence.[8]

Self-Awareness
- Observe the impact of your emotions on others.
- Pay attention to emotions you seek to avoid.
- Feel where in your body your emotions express themselves.
- Know who and what pushes your buttons.
- Keep a journal of your emotions.
- Get to know yourself under stress, both what you feel and what you tell yourself.

Self-Management
- Learn the power of breathing.
- Count to ten.
- Sleep on it.
- Replace negative self-talk with positive self-talk.
- Get quality sleep.

7. Bradberry and Greaves, *Emotional Intelligence 2.0*, 32–39.
8. Bradberry and Greaves, *Emotional Intelligence 2.0*. These strategies are found on pages 61–175.

- Exercise.
- Expect change to come.

Social Awareness
- Greet people by name.
- Watch body language.
- Plan ahead for social gatherings.
- Learn to listen.
- Put yourself in the other person's shoes.
- Catch the mood of the room.

You will need to develop friendships inside and outside the seminary to support your vocation. You will also need to be able to relate well with others to engage in ministry. Both of these features of seminary life depend on your developing the skills of self-awareness, self-management, and social awareness. In every friendship and ministry situation, you must be aware of your emotions and be able to read the emotional state of those who come to you for friendship and ministry. You will be able to develop relationships by drawing on your self-awareness and your awareness of others to communicate and bond with them. The following are strategies you can use when developing relationships with family, friends, and in ministry:

- Be open and curious.
- Match body language and voice tone with message.
- Build trust.
- Remember that little things matter.
- Acknowledge the other person's emotions.

Implemented Intentions and Good Habits

Another way you can participate in your own growth in formation is by adopting two practices that are backed up by years of research by cognitive psychologists. The first involves implementing intentions. This process can be used for *short-term goals*. Discovered and developed by psychologist Peter Gollwitzer of New York University, the practice of implementing intentions is a powerful way of ensuring you will carry out new goals and intentions that come up throughout the formation process. Whether it be a new goal for studies, exercise, prayer, nutrition, or ministry, the process developed by Professor Gollwitzer is proven to put intentions into practice so they become a habit. The secret is to identify a future time, place, and way that a goal will be carried out. For instance, when trying to get a group of elderly people to take the various pills in the pillbox, researchers suggested they take pill 1 immediately after breakfast and pill 4 at bedtime right before turning out the light. Several months later the group had a 100 percent adherence rate. The same process was used for making doctor appointments, with voters, and with people who sought to avoid a temptation related to food. For instance, the dieters told themselves "The next time I am tempted to eat chocolate I will think of my diet." Researchers found this process was far more successful than willpower. The reason is that by linking the intended goal to a time and place, the person had an external cue that made the practice automatic. Brain imaging studies have shown that when implementation intention is employed, control over behavior shifts from the self-initiated part of the brain to the part of the brain stimulated by the outside environment.[9]

Professor John Bargh reported using this method as a way of protecting his family from the frustrations of his workday. He succeeded in doing this by deciding that when he gets out of his car before entering the house, he would be happy he was home and about to be greeted by his family.[10] This is a powerful tool you can use to make changes in each dimension of formation. The important point is to identify the specific goal you want to achieve and the time and place where it will be implemented.

The second approach involves a method for developing *good life-long habits*. These life-long habits include prayer, study, exercise, nutrition, and taking a day off that will help you live a healthy and holy life as a priest. Research shows that the best way to do this is to form good habits that are connected to a concrete place and time. Adopting a new practice, such as exercise, can be difficult, but by developing a regular routine, new neural pathways grow, gradually making it easier. As these pathways strengthen through regular practice, the new practice becomes a habit. The good news is that the habit soon becomes automatic and your behavior is driven by habit and not willpower. Researchers at the University of Pennsylvania found regular habits make an activity effortless, whether it be exercise, study, or

9.   Peter Gollwitzer, "Implementation Intentions: Strong Effects of Simple Plans," *American Psychologist* 54, no. 7 (1999): 493–503.

10.   Bargh, *Before You Know It,* 273–74.

any other practice. The trick is to set up one's environment so that it is easy to engage in the new habit. For instance, setting out the breviary the night before so you pray it first thing in the morning, associating study with morning coffee, or setting out running shoes and shorts the night before are all prompts that make a new practice easier and can turn it into a habit. By setting up the environment and making an implementation intention, the new practice soon becomes automatic.[11]

Reflection on Pastoral Practice

The most concrete way you can participate in the formation process is through your various pastoral ministry experiences. During seminary, you will be involved in the following kinds of ministry: ministry with the poor, catechesis, hospital ministry, and parish ministry. While time consuming, ministry will often be the most rewarding part of your week. It can give you a sense of actively contributing to the ministry of the Church and bringing some good into people's lives.

Learning to reflect on these pastoral experiences is another important way you can participate in your formation. As mentioned above, the practice of pausing to

---

11. Bargh, *Before You Know It*, 275–78; B. M. Galla & A. L. Duckworth, "More than Resisting Temptation: Beneficial Habits Mediate Relationships between Self-control and Positive Life Outcomes," *Journal of Personality and Social Psychology* 109, no. 3 (2015): 508–25.

THE POWER OF PARTICIPATION 79

reflect on ministry experiences is not a natural habit in our task-oriented world that is focused on the next thing. Often, much more was happening in your experience of ministry both for you and those you serve than you may, at first, realize.

The following questions can help you reflect on your ministry experience. Be sure to share your insights with your formator.

- Progress: How is your ministry going thus far? What kinds of things are you doing? Let's consider a particular event.
- Gratitude: Looking back on your ministry experience, who and what you are you grateful to God for?
- Mood: What mood were you in as the experience started? What feelings and desires emerged during it and afterwards?
- Pastoral practice: What went well? How did the people you serve experience your presence, words, and actions?
- The action of God: Where did you find God in this experience?
- Next time: Any other ways to improve how you serve God's people?

Reflection on Preaching

The purpose of seminary formation is to train you for the life and ministry of the parish priesthood. If you are ordained a priest, you will preach almost every day and each weekend.

[12] You will become a professional preacher. As countless surveys have shown, the people in the pew long for better preaching. Learning to reflect on your experience of preaching is essential to becoming a good preacher who can proclaim the Gospel in engaging and meaningful ways that transforms lives. This kind of reflection should happen while you are enrolled in preaching courses, not only with your classmates but with your formator. This can lead to a conversation about how to prepare for a homily, how you felt while preaching, what you hoped to achieve, and what response you received from your professor and classmates. The process can be overwhelming and discouraging at first so I suggest you select one area of the preaching process to work on per semester to improve your preaching. If you do this, in a few years you will be a different preacher! Once you are ordained a deacon, you will be preaching with some regularity in the parish. Reflecting on these experiences can be very fruitful as well. The following questions can guide some of this discussion.

- In a sentence, what was your message? What were you hoping the people heard?
- How did you feel while preaching?
- How was your eye contact? Were the people paying attention or were heads down?

---

12. A helpful resource for reflecting on different dimensions of preaching is Deacon Edward McCormack, "Ten Commandments for Transformative Preaching," *Homiletic and Pastoral Review*, November 29, 2015. Found at www.hprweb.com.

- Describe your preparation process.
- How was your delivery?
- What feedback did you receive? What aspect of preaching do you want to work on improving this semester?

5 | Evaluations

BEGINNING IN FEBRUARY, the formation faculty starts the process of writing evaluations for each seminarian that will be sent to your bishop. Your formator will write an evaluation that will review your formational progress during the year indicating where growth has occurred and what areas of formation to focus on in the next year. This evaluation is reviewed and approved by the entire faculty. He will also ask you to write a self-evaluation, which your advisor and the formation faculty will read. What follows are some guidelines for writing the self-evaluation, a style sheet, and sample evaluation.

Guidelines for the Annual Seminarian Self-Evaluation

Your self-evaluation involves reflecting and writing about your formation experience since you entered seminary this year in terms of the four dimensions of formation: human, spiritual, intellectual, and pastoral. Before you write your evaluation, take some time to consider the primary issues you have been discussing with your advisor. Where have you been challenged to grow and where do you feel you have made some progress? Where is further growth called for?

After reflecting on all that has happened to you since the beginning of the academic year, write up the results of your reflection, discussing each area of formation. Your self-evaluation should reflect where you have noticed and experienced growth in each of the four areas of formation, as well as insight into further need for growth. It should exhibit a growing self-knowledge, especially regarding those areas in your life where growth is called for. The following style sheet should guide your writing.

Style Sheet

Software:	Microsoft Word
Margins:	1" margins on all sides of the document
Font size:	12 point
Font	Times New Roman (on all text)
Paragraphs:	No indentations (Use block style on everything)
Spacing:	Single spacing
Subheadings:	**Bold subheadings**. Do not bold any text.
Paragraph	No indentation, flush left
Page Numbers:	Centered – bottom of each page
Length:	Ordinary Evaluations: ordinarily about 2 ½ - 3 pages
Major Evaluations: ordinarily about 3–4 pages

Self-Evaluation Format

Samuel Spade Self-Evaluation

Archdiocese of Somewhere
1st Pre-Theology
Spring, 1500

Human and Spiritual Development

In this section, describe the relationships that sustain you and your participation in seminary committees, activities and organizations as well as activities outside the seminary.

Discuss the primary human formation issues you worked on this year. Identify insights gained and where growth occurred in human formation this year. Also discuss areas of ongoing growth.

Discuss the primary spiritual formation issues you focused on this year. Include a list of your regular spiritual practices. Discuss how your relationship with God developed this year and say a few words about the status of your vocational discernment.

Diaconate

If you are preparing for ordination to the diaconate, include at the end of the section on spiritual formation a few words on your readiness and desire to be a deacon. Explain your understanding of and readiness to live the promises you will make at your ordination. This should include celibacy, Liturgy of the Hours/ a life of prayer, obedience, and simplicity of life. Each public commitment should be reflected on separately (e.g., how do you understand the importance of celibacy and what leads you to believe you are ready to commit to it and how do you understand the importance of Liturgy of the Hours.)

Priesthood

If you are preparing for ordination to the ministerial priesthood, include at the end of the section on spiritual formation a reflection on your experience of the diaconate and how it has prepared you for priesthood, and if you feel ready to assume the new ministries of priesthood. Say a few words about your ability to preach, the ministerial skills you have developed, and those you still need to develop.

Intellectual and Pastoral Development

Discuss your intellectual development this year, indicating the degree programs you are enrolled in as well as your GPA. Discuss the courses that were meaningful to you and those that were challenging. Say a few words about how any of your courses offered insight into the meaning of the Christian faith and the practice of ministry.

Discuss your experience of ministry this year. Include a discussion of any joys and struggles, what you learned about this ministry, what ministerial challenges came up, and what pastoral skills you developed.

Selected Bibliography

Magisterial and Sulpician Documents on Formation for Priestly Ministry

Vatican Council II. *Optatam totius*. October 28, 1965.

———. *Presbyterorum ordinis*. December 7, 1965.

John Paul II. *Pastores Dabo Vobis*. Washington, DC: Office for Publishing and Promotion Services, United States Catholic Conference, 1992.

Congregation for the Clergy. *The Gift of the Priestly Vocation: Ratio Fundamentalis Institutionis Sacerdotalis*. December 8, 2016.

Committee on Priestly Formation of the United States Conference of Catholic Bishops. *Program of Priestly Formation*. 5th ed. Washington, DC: USCCB Publishing, 2006.

Marks of a Sulpician Seminary. Society of St. Sulpice, Province of the USA, 1994.

Witherup, Ronald D., PSS, ed. *The Sulpicians: A Tradition of Priestly Formation*. Paris: Society of the Priests of Saint Sulpice, 2013.

Celibacy

Aschenbrenner, George, SJ. *Quickening the Fire in Our Midst: The Challenge of Diocesan Priestly Spirituality*. Chicago: Loyola Press, 2002.

Bleichner, Howard, Daniel Buechlein, and Robert Leavitt. *Celibacy for the Kingdom: Theological Reflections and Practical Perspectives*. Rev. ed. Baltimore: St. Mary's Seminary and University, 1990. Criterion Press, 1997.

Congregation for the Clergy. *The Gift of the Priestly Vocation: Ratio Fundamentalis Institutionis Sacerdotalis*. December 8, 2016.

Cavadini, John C., ed. *The Charism of Priestly Celibacy: Biblical, Theological, and Pastoral Reflections*. Institute for Church Life. Notre Dame, IN: Ave Maria Press, 2012

Dolan, Bishop Timothy M. *Priests for the Third Millennium*. Huntington, IN: Our Sunday Visitor Publishers, 2000. See esp. chap. 17 and 23.

John Paul II. *Pastores Dabo Vobis*. Washington, DC: Office for Publishing and Promotion Services, United States Catholic Conference, 1992.

Manuel, Gerdenio Sonny, SJ. "Living Chastity; Psychosexual Well-Being in Jesuit Life." *Studies in the Spirituality of Jesuits* 41, no. 2 (Summer 2009).

Paul VI. *Sacerdotalis Caelibatus: Encyclical of Pope Paul VI on the Celibacy of the Priest*. June 24, 1967. http://w2.vatican.va/content/paul-vi/en/encyclicals.index.html.

Sacred Congregation for Catholic Education. *A Guide to Formation in Priestly Celibacy*. Rome, 1974.

Selin, Gary. *Priestly Celibacy: Theological Foundations.* Washington, DC: The Catholic University of America Press, 2016.

For the Sake of the Kingdom: A Sulpician Approach to Formation in Priestly Celibacy. Paris: The Society of the Priests of St. Sulpice, 2005.

Vatican Council II. *Presbyterorum ordinis.* December 7, 1965.

Common Formation Issues

Adult Children of Alcohols (Association). *Adult Children of Alcoholics: Alcoholic and Dysfunctional Families.* Torrance, CA: World Service Organization, Inc., 2006.

> The comprehensive text on all the issues adult children face. This book is not just for children from homes of alcoholics. It is filled with great insights into many formation issues formators find seminarians deal with as well as ways to help them.

Bargh, John. *Before You Know It.* New York: Touchstone, 2017.

Blanchette, Melvin, PSS. "Negotiating the Pillars of Formation." An unpublished document.

> A wonderful guide to the various issues a formator should discuss with his advisees at each stage of formation taking into account the four pillars.

Bradberry, Travis, and Jean Greaves. *Emotional Intelligence 2.0.* San Diego, CA: TalentSmart Publishers, 2009.

> This book lays out in simple language the four skills of emotional intelligence: self-awareness, self-management, social awareness, and relationship management. It comes with an online test to gauge your emotional quotient and examples of

high and low skilled people and strategies for growing all four skills.

Brooks, David. *The Social Animal: The Hidden Sources of
Love, Character, and Achievement*. New York: Random House, 2012.

An engaging and eye-opening survey of recent
insights into relationships and human development
from the field of neuroscience.

———. *The Road to Character*. New York: Random House,
2015.

Cain, Susan. *Quiet: The Power of Introverts in a World that
Can't Stop Talking*. New York: Broadway Books, 2013.

A ground-breaking book on the power of introverts, silence, solitude, and creativity in a world that
privileges extroverts and group brain storming.
Very important for advising since many seminarians are introverts.

Dweck, Carol. *Mindset: The New Psychology of Success: How
We Can Learn to Fulfill Our Potential*. New York:
Ballantine Books, 2006.

Sets out on the impact of a "fixed mindset" com-
pared to a "growth mindset" on various dimensions
of life. This book is can help formators promote a
growth mindset within the men they guide.

Jay, Meg. *The Defining Decade. Why Your Twenties Matter
and How to Make the Most of Them Now*. New York:
Twelve, 2013.

An important book for advisors who are working with men in their twenties. Filled with insights
into what is happening developmentally at this age
and what is needed for them to grow and mature.

Horney, Karen. *Neurosis and Human Growth: The Struggle Toward Self-Realization.* New York: W. W. Norton and Company, reissued in 1991. Esp. chap. 3, "The Tyranny of the Should," and chap. 5, "Self-Hate and Self-Contempt."

McBrearity, Gerald, PSS. "Spiritual Development." *Seminary News* 32, no. 3 (1994).

Newberg, Andrew. *Words Can Change Your Brain: Twelve Conversation Strategies to Build Trust, Resolve Conflict and Increase Intimacy.* New York: Plume Publishing, 2013.

> Combining the insights of neuroscience and communication studies, these authors offer seminarians twelve strategies for compassionate communication.

Smith, James K. A. *Desiring the Kingdom: Worship, Worldview and Cultural Formation,* Volume 1 Grand Rapids: Baker Academic, 2009; *Imagining the Kingdom: How Worship Works,* Volume 2. 2013.

Stein, Steven J., and Howard E. Book, MD. *The EQ Edge: Emotional Intelligence and your Success.* Mississauga, ON: Jossey-Bass, 2011.

Diet and Nutrition

Fuhrman, Joel. *The End of Heart Disease: The Eat to Live Plan to Prevent and Reverse Heart Disease.* New York: HarperOne Books, 2016.

> A readable and compelling book on healthy eating.

Fung, Jason. *The Obesity Code: Unlocking the Secrets of Weight Loss.* Berkeley: Greystone Books, 2016.

Perhaps the most important book you will read on nutrition with a focus on the cause of obesity. The book debunks many of our assumptions regarding weight loss and diet including the dominant belief that less calories, less fat, and more exercise leads to weight loss. The book makes a powerful evidence-based claim citing many studies that it is the increase in insulin and insulin resistance that lead to weight gain. The last two chapters offer clear guidelines as to what to eat and when to eat. This is a very valuable book as many seminarians face issues with their weight.

Hyman, Mark. *Eat Fat Get Thin: Why the Fat We Eat is the Key to Sustained Weight Loss and Vibrant Health*. New York: Little, Brown, Spark, 2016.

Hyman, a well-known author and doctor at the Cleveland Clinic, turns forty years of diet advice on its head. For years, we have been told fat makes you fat when it turns out there is no scientific evidence to back up this claim. What makes us fat is the consumption of refined carbohydrates that cause dramatic rise in insulin. The consumption of healthy fat fills us up and does not cause a spike in insulin. This is a very readable book based on the latest research. It comes with list of good food to eat and recipes.

Ludwig, David. *Always Hungry: Conquer Cravings, Retrain Fat Cells, and Lose Weight Permanently*. New York: Grand Central Life & Style, 2016.

Harvard researcher David Ludwig debunks the belief that eating fat makes us fat while promoting a diet of healthy fats, protein, and carbs that avoids the real dangers of processed foods and refined carbs. The book includes menus and recipes.

Mosely, Michael, and Mimi Spencer. *The FastDiet: Lose Weight, Stay Healthy, Live Longer by Simple Secret of Intermittent Fasting.* Rev. ed. New York: Atria Books, 2015.

An excellent book on the importance of intermittent fasting for weight loss.

Discernment

Gallagher, Timothy. *The Discernment of Spirits: An Ignatian Guide for Everyday Living.* New York: Crossroad, 2005.

A practical guide through St. Ignatius of Loyola's first set of rules on discerning spirits. This is a very readable book packed with wisdom about the spiritual life, Ignatian spirituality based on the best scholarship. Gallagher presents Ignatius "Rules" along with case studies. This is an invaluable text for spiritual directors and advisors.

———. *The Examen Prayer.* New York: Crossroad Publishing, 2006.

Gallagher presents St. Ignatius of Loyola's classic prayer the *Examen* in a way that brings it to life by showing how this prayer captures the fundamental features of our relationship with Christ.

———, *Discerning the Will of God: An Ignatian Guide to Christian Decision Making.* New York: Crossroad, 2009.

A clear presentation using case studies of the three Ignatian methods of discerning God's will.

An essential text for spiritual directors and advisors who are helping a man discern his vocation.

Hahnenberg, Edward. *Awakening Vocation: A Theology of Christian Call.* Collegeville, MN: Liturgical Press, 2010.

A dense and insightful contemporary theology of vocation drawing on the riches of our Christian tradition.

Haughey, John, SJ. *Revisiting the Idea of Vocation: Theological Explorations.* Washington, DC: The Catholic University of America Press, 2012.

Parish Life and Leadership

Byron, William J., SJ. *Parish Leadership: Principles and Practices.* Lakewood, NJ: Clear Faith Publishing, 2017.

Jesuit William Byron discusses the importance of shared leadership as servant leadership rather than the corrupting to down approach. He also discusses the importance of introducing Catholic social teaching into parish life.

Heath, Chip, and Dan Heath. *Switch: How to Change Things When Change is Hard.* New York: Broadway Books, 2010.

The Heath brothers bring together years of research in a story-driven narrative about how cultures, institutions, and persons can change.

Kouzes, James M., and Barry Z. Posner. *The Leadership Challenge: How to Make Extraordinary Things Happen in Organizations.* Fifth Edition. San Francisco: Jossey-Bass, 2012.

Mallon, James. *Divine Renovation: Bringing Your Parish from Maintenance to Mission*. New London, CT: Twenty-Third Publications, 2014.

Roxburgh, Alan J., and Fred Romanuk. *The Missional Leader: Equipping Your Church to Reach a Changing World*. San Francisco: Jossey-Bass, 2006.

Sipp, James W., and Don M. Frick. *Seven Pillars of Servant Leadership: Practicing the Wisdom of Leading by Serving*. Mahwah, NJ: Paulist Press, 2015.

Simon, William E. *Great Catholic Parishes: A Living Mosaic— How Four Essential Practices Make Them Thrive*. Notre Dame, IN: Ave Maria Press, 2016.

White, Michael. *Rebuilt: Awakening the Faithful, Reaching the Lost, and Making Church Matter*. Notre Dame, IN: Ave Maria Press, 2013.

> White, a priest from the Archdiocese of Baltimore, tells the story of bringing a dying parish back to life and transforming it into a parish that matters to people's lives. An essential read for all fourth-year seminarians.

———. *Tools for Rebuilding: 75 Really, Really Practical Ways to Make Your Parish Better*. Notre Dame, IN: Ave Maria Press, 2013.

> The follow up to *Rebuilt*. This book is filled with wonderful and concrete suggestions for bringing our parishes to life.

Preaching

Heath, Chip, and Dan Heath. *Made to Stick: Why Some Ideas Survive and Others Die*. New York: Random House, 2008.

These authors present a tested method for developing a message that sticks to the imagination of people. These authors advocate for SUCCES: Simple, Unexpected, Concrete, Clear, Emotional Stories approach to presentations. Every preacher should read this book.

McCormack, Deacon Edward. "Ten Commandments for Transformative Preaching." *Homiletic & Pastoral Review* (http:/www.hprweb.com/). November 29, 2015.

A concrete guide to preaching in a way that connects Scripture to the lives of the people in order to promote transformation.

Stanley, Andy, and Lane Jones. *Communicating for a Change*. Colorado Springs: Multnomah Books, 2006.

This may be the most important book any seminarian reads about preaching. The authors propose as the goal of preaching transformation rather than information. With this goal in mind, Stanley and Lane direct the preacher to pick one message and build their homily around it using a relational model of preaching. This model starts with where the people are, interprets that situation through Scripture and concludes by showing how to put the message into practice.

Untener, Kenneth. *Preaching Better: Practical Suggestions for Homilists*. Mahwah, NJ: Paulist Press, 1999.

A classic that covers the fundamentals of preparing and delivering a homily. Each chapter begins with wisdom from the people who listen to our preaching. It is a gold mine!

Wallace, James. *Preaching to the Hungers of the Heart: The Homily on the Feasts and within the Rites.* Collegeville, MN: Liturgical Press, 2002.
    Written by a master professor of homiletics, this book offers practical wisdom for anyone preaching with special attention to feast days, various church seasons, Mary, and the sacraments.

Priesthood

Aschenbrenner, George, SJ. *Quickening the Fire in Our Midst: The Challenge of Diocesan Priestly Spirituality.* Chicago: Loyola Press, 2002.
    Based on Aschenbrenner's experience as a spiritual director at the North American College and founder of IPF, this book describes the different dimensions of diocesan spirituality that can be very helpful for seminarians.

Buckley, Michael. "Importance of Weakness in the Priesthood: A Letter to the Ordinands [Jesuits about to be Ordained]." *The Berkeley Jesuit* (Spring 1972): 8.

Congar, Yves. *A Gospel Priesthood.* Translated by P. J. Hepburne-Scott. New York: Herder and Herder, 1967.
    Chapters 6, 8, 9, 10, and 11 offer a goldmine of insights into the priesthood from one of our great theologians.

Hahnenberg, Edward P. *Ministries: A Relational Approach.* New York: Herder & Herder, 2003.
    An important theological study of ordained ministry. In critical dialogue with the tradition

and building on the insights of Vatican II, the work proposes that ordained ministry be set within the context of the Christian community and seen as a permanent and public commitment to service to that community. What changes for the ordained is his relationship to the community and the public and permanent service he offers that community. The book contains rich and practical insights for ordained ministry.

Power, Dermot. *A Spiritual Theology of the Priesthood: The Mystery of Christ and the Mission of the Priest.* Washington, DC: The Catholic University of America Press, 1998.

Rolheiser, Ronald. *Sacred Fire: A Vision for a Deeper Human and Christian Maturity.* New York: Random House, 2014.

Written by a master of the spiritual life, Rolheiser sets out the spiritual life in terms of three moments in human development: the effort to get our lives together; the challenge of giving our lives away; and finally, giving our deaths away. Rolheiser draws on Scripture and the wisdom of the Christian spiritual tradition to describe these three movements. This book is filled with rich insights into the spiritual life that are particularly relevant to seminary formation since that process compresses the first two moments and challenges the men to move into and through both as they head towards ordination.

Index